Making Working Wooden Locks

Making Working Wooden Locks

Complete Plans For 5 Working Wooden Locks

Tim Detweiler

LINDEN PUBLISHING
FRESNO, CA

Making Working Wooden Locks

by

Tim Detweiler

© 2000 by Tim Detweiler
ISBN 0-941936-60-0

2 4 6 8 9 7 5 3

Library of Congress Cataloging-in-Publication Data

Detweiler, Tim, 1931-
    Making working wooden locks / by Tim Detweiler.-- 1st ed.
      p. cm. -- (Woodworker's library)
    ISBN 0-941936-60-0
    1. Woodwork, 2. Wooden locks. I. Title. II. Woodworker's library (Fresno, Calif.)

TT200 .D48 2000
684.08--dc21   00-041237

LINDEN PUBLISHING

The Woodworker's Library

Linden Publishing Inc.
2006 S.Mary
Fresno, CA 93721 USA
tel 800-345-4447
www.lindenpub.com

Printed and bound in Singapore

Table of Contents

top:
Antique lever lock, ash and walnut, 10"x16".

center:
Pin tumbler lock, 82 pieces of walnut and maple, 10"x16".

bottom:
Combination lock with four number combination, English oak burl and walnut, 10"x16", 10 lbs.

Part I:

Acknowledgments

First I want to thank Darrell Rhoades, as he was the first to tell me that if I ever made wooden locks to sell, he wanted some. Then credit has to go to my wife, Charlene, for letting me spend so much time in the shop, and helping to sell my locks at art and craft shows. Thanks also to the many people at the shows who said they would buy a book if I had one published. Special thanks goes to my son, Phil, for putting the drawings on the computer, and last and most of all, for the beautiful work she did typing all this on the computer, I thank my daughter-in-law, Carlyn.

— *Tim Detweiler, "The Lock Man"*

Dedication

First of all, I want to give my father much of the credit for this book. As a young boy I was never discouraged from trying to make something from wood. During the Depression in the 1930s, I learned at an early age to make do with what was available, which was not much. This helped me to learn the importance of not wasting materials. My father always said that whatever you make, make it the best you possibly can. Make it as good as if you were going to keep it for yourself.

Now I am a grandfather of wonderful twin grandsons, Erick and Matthew.

To them I dedicate this book with love.

Introduction

This book is being produced as a way of passing on to other craftsmen a craft that, to my knowledge, no one else has ever done. This is the craft of constructing working padlocks made entirely of wood. I designed and made these locks as a challenge to myself to produce such a lock using no metal parts. In the following chapters, you will be taken step by step through the making of several different kinds of padlocks. We will start with the easiest, a warded lock, and work up to the more challenging locks.

First let me tell you how all this started. I was born in 1931, during the Depression, about 200 miles north of Detroit, Michigan. We had very few toys in those days. A block of wood, with a little imagination, would become a bulldozer or maybe a truck. As the years passed, the toys and other projects, such as birdhouses, were made with a little more skill. In 1942 we moved to Dayton, Ohio, where in junior and senior high school I made many wooden projects in woodshop classes and also at home. I have worked in construction as a carpenter and custom homebuilder all my working life. In 1982, I took a correspondence course in locksmithing. I worked part-time at locksmithing for fourteen years and full-time for ten years as a service manager for a large construction company before retiring in 1995. In the summer of 1988 I designed the first lock that we will make. I made twenty-seven locks, not knowing if I could sell even a single one. They did begin to sell, so next I designed a combination lock with a three-number combination, which will be the second lock we will make. Other kinds of locks will follow in later chapters.

In November 1988, I participated in the "Artistry in Wood" show in Dayton, Ohio, to see if I could sell my wooden padlocks to the public. I not only sold locks, but also won "Best of Show" in woodworking with a wooden plate that I had entered into competition. For the next ten years, my wife and I exhibited our locks at fine art and craft shows all across the country. We have participated in about ninety shows, and no one has disputed my claim that I am the only one making all-wood padlocks. As of January 1999 I have made 3,500 wooden padlocks.

In October 1990 there was a very good article written about my locks by Dana Dunn. The article appeared in *Woodshop News*. In the July 1997 issue of *The National Locksmith*, there was an excellent article about my work by Jake Jakubuwski, who is the technical editor. This publication is distributed to locksmiths around the world. As a result, we have shipped wooden padlocks all over the United States and to at least nine foreign countries.

I hope that you will be encouraged to try your hand at making these locks. They are an excellent project for the person who wants to make something different. When you give one of these locks as a gift to a two-year-old or a ninety-two year old, it is a joy to see their faces light up and their eyes sparkle.

Chapter One
Materials

First let us consider the kinds of wood to be used in making a wooden lock. Almost any solid wood can be used for the body of the lock. I have used wood all the way from old barn boards to imported, exotic, and colorful woods such as padauk, wenge, tiger wood, zebrawood, purple heart, lacewood, bocote, pear, and teak. I prefer hardwoods, as they are much stronger and usually more colorful than softwoods, but you can even use plywood in making some of the pieces. Always use good, dry wood or you will have problems with shrinking, warping, and cracking that at the very least will make the lock look bad and at the very worst prevent the lock from working at all.

The woods used for making the shackles and keys must be straight-grained hardwood. I use mostly ash, maple, oak, walnut, and cherry.

All the keyed locks that we discuss in this book use wooden springs. The spring was one of my biggest problems to overcome in making an all-wood keyed lock. I take extremely straight-grained ash as my first choice and hickory as a close second choice. Both woods cut well with a sharp saw and are springy and very tough. When you have selected the woods you are going to use, lay out and make patterns if necessary for such parts as the shackle and key.

With all locks, be precise with your measurements, as they will greatly affect how the lock works. Carefully follow the step-by-step instructions. As you work on the different pieces, go slowly and test-fit them as you proceed. When all the pieces are made, clamp (do not glue) them together, and try the key or combination to make sure that the lock works properly. I recommend that you start with the warded lock in Chapter Five, as it is the easiest to make.

Chapter Two
Shop Safety Tips

Shop safety is always the first concern of the craftsman. I cannot stress the importance of being careful. Even the most skilled and experienced craftsmen can tell you stories about how they made a mistake and were either hurt or came very close to being hurt.

Please keep in mind the following safety tips:

1. Never wear loose or baggy clothes. Keep shirt-tails tucked in, long baggy sleeves rolled up, and do not wear a necktie.

2. Keep your shop clean. Keep all pieces of wood out of walkways and under the workbench or in racks and boxes.

3. When you walk away from a tool or machine, turn it off.

4. Always follow the tool manufacturer's safety tips when using a tool.

5. Use sharp tools. A dull tool is far more dangerous and harder to use.

6. Dust is a major concern. Some woods are toxic when the dust is inhaled. Use a facemask when sawing or sanding.

7. Ventilation of your shop is important when applying finishes. Follow instructions on the container.

8. Do not allow children in the shop.

9. If someone talks to you, stop working. The loss of attention is a certain road to injury.

Chapter Three
Tools

You do not have to be an expert woodworker with all the latest and best tools to be successful in making a wooden lock. You can start with the tools listed under "basic" and substitute "intermediate" or "advanced" as available.

Basic Tools

1. Sharp handsaw

2. Coping saw

3. 6-inch clamps

4. Wood plane

5. Wood rasps and files

6. Brace and bits: 1/4" to 1-3/4"

7. Carpenter's wood glue

8. Sandpaper: 60 to 220 grit

Intermediate Tools

1. 3/8" variable-speed electric drill

2. Set of 1/4" to 2-1/8" Forstner wood bits*

3. Electric miter saw

4. Belt sander

5. Bench vise

6. Router

Advanced Tools

1. Table saw

2. Band saw

3. Drill press

4. Bench belt sander

5. Turning lathe

Look at your tool purchases as lifetime investments. When you buy a tool, buy the best you can afford, as it will serve you longer and better.

When drilling holes to a certain depth, use a small tape measure. Drill slowly and measure as needed to get the right depth. You can use a small stick or nail to check the depth, measuring how far it goes into the hole.

*Note: Forstner wood bits bore flat-bottomed holes. A set of them will make lock-making much easier.

Chapter Four
Finishing

Sanding your lock in preparation for applying the finish is a very important part of crafting a high-quality project. Start with 60-grit sandpaper for very rough surfaces and edges and work up to the final sanding with 220 grit. Always sand with the wood grain, not across it.

I recommend using a vacuum cleaner to remove dust from the lock, followed by wiping with a tack cloth to prepare for the finish.

Much has been written about finishes in other books and articles. I will not discuss all the different finishes or how to apply them. I have used many different finishes and it is my conclusion that the best finish for a wooden lock is a good grade of polyurethane. My preferred method of applying the finish is with 2" foam brushes, but you can use another method if you choose. I recommend that you do not attempt to spray on the finish, as it will get into the lock and probably ruin it. Follow the directions on the finish container for best results.

Part II:
The Projects

counter-clockwise from top:

Warded lock with key, pg. 14
Three-number combination lock, pg. 28
Antique lever lock, pg. 44
Railroad switch lock, pg. 58
Antique push key lever lock, pg. 76

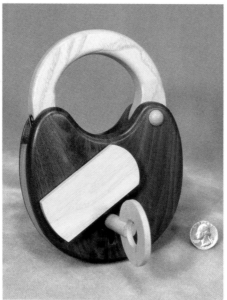

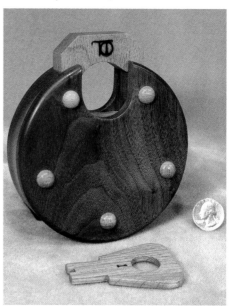

About the Drawings

The projects in this book are drawn using basic drafting techniques. Objects are drawn on three standard views: front, top, and side. These multiple views help give a clearer idea of the object's structure and dimensions. Not all views are used in every drawing; only those which best illustrate the object. The drawings are shown full-size whenever possible, so you can trace them from the book and use them as plans.

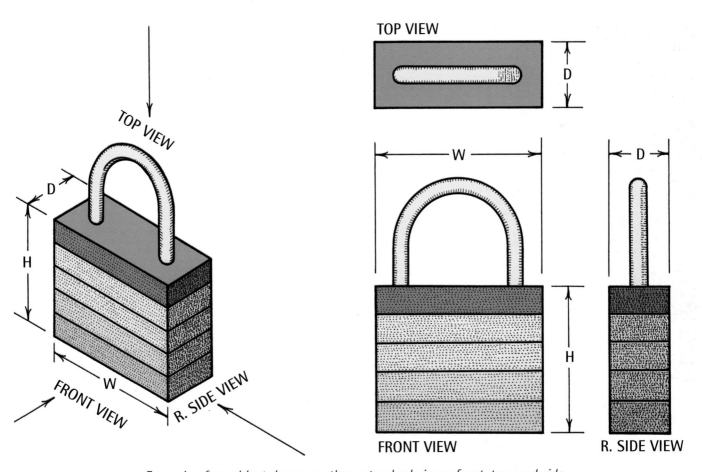

Example of an object drawn on three standard views: front, top, and side.

Chapter Five
Warded Lock with Key

The first thing to do is to select the kind of wood that you are going to use to make your lock. The easiest wood to work with if you do not have power tools is white pine or possibly poplar. Walnut, cherry, ash, and many other hardwoods are stronger and more colorful, but are more difficult to work by hand. Five or six different kinds of wood make a beautiful lock.

STEP 1

Cut out five pieces of wood 3/4" thick, 2-1/4" wide, and 4 1/2" long. These will be stacked to make the lock body. When all five pieces are cut to size, number them one through five and mark the top of each piece, as in Figure 1.

If you have a drill press I suggest that you make a platform (Figure 2) with stops along one side and a positioning stop at one end. Clamp the platform on the drill-press base so you can move it to the proper location for drilling. Make the length to fit your own drill press.

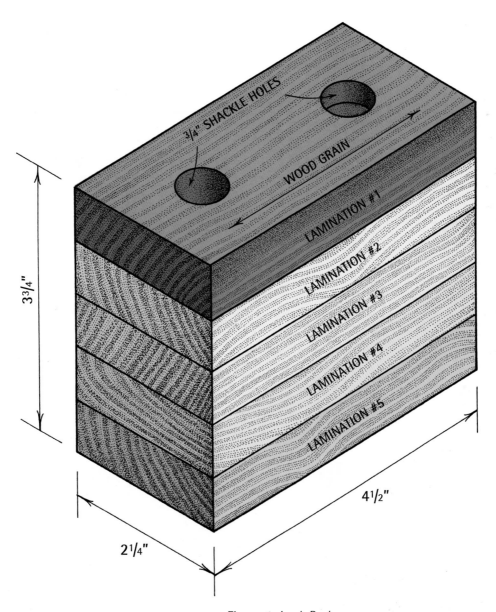

Figure 1. Lock Body.

STEP 2

Position the platform so that the 3/4" hole at one end of lamination #1 is exactly in the right location. Use a piece of scrap wood the same size as a lock lamination to check hole location. Once centered, you can drill all holes at either end of all five laminations without moving your setup. Be careful to use the right drill size for each hole.

STEP 3

All holes must be drilled straight into the wood. Lay out all holes on the top and bottom of lamination #1 as shown in Figure 3.

STEP 4

Drill the 3/4" shackle hole "A" all the way through lamination #1.

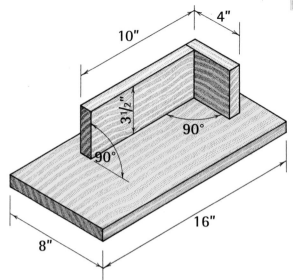

Figure 2. Drilling platform.

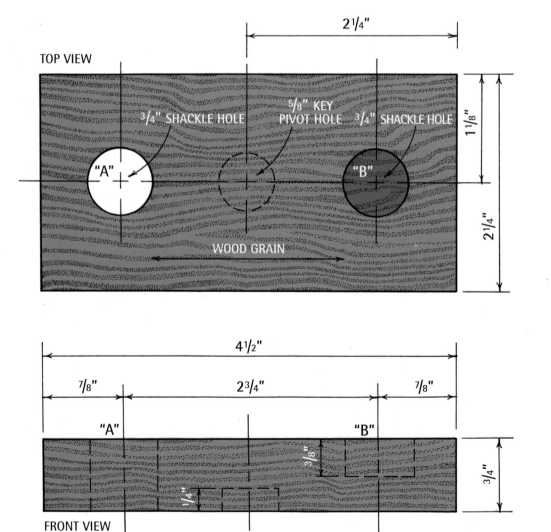

Figure 3. Lamination #1 (top of lock). Scale = full-size.

STEP 5

Turn the lamination around in the jig and drill the 3/4" shackle hole "B" 3/8" deep.

STEP 6

Use a 5/8" bit to drill the key pivot hole 1/4" deep in the exact center of the bottom of lamination #1.

STEP 7

Lay out the shaded area and the two angled cuts for mounting the springs on lamination #2 (Figure 4).

STEP 8

Drill a 1/2" hole in the shaded area for the sawblade. Cut out the shaded area in Figure 4 with a saber saw or jig-saw. This cutout is not critical, but do not make the hole too big or too small.

STEP 9

I use a saber saw to make the two cuts that hold the wood springs. You can use a handsaw but be very careful in either case to get the angle of cut right. This angle is what puts tension on the springs so that the springs snap into the locking notches in the shackle when the lock is closed. Please note in Figure 4 that the springs are 3/8" apart at the free end on the left. As I stated before, these cuts are critical. If there is not enough of an angle, the lock may not lock; if too much of an angle, the lock will not operate easily or, worse yet, the springs may break when the key is turned.

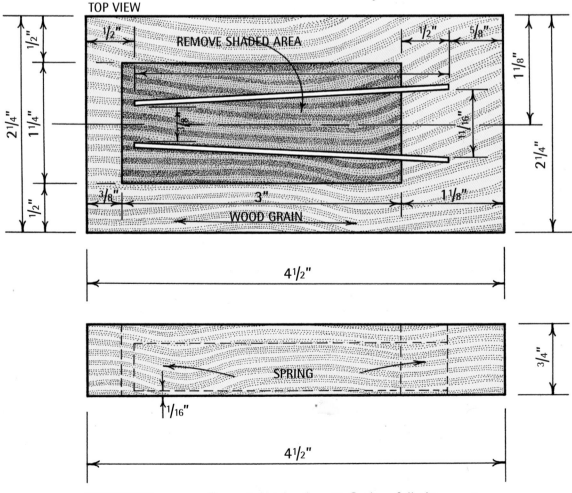

FRONT VIEW   *Figure 4. Lamination #2. Scale = full-size.*

STEP 10

To make the springs, select a piece of ash or hickory. These woods have very straight grain. I use a table saw with a 40- or 50-tooth blade to saw my springs, but you can use other tools to make yours. You must end up with two pieces that are 1/16" thick, 1/2" wide, and 3-3/8" long. Now test-fit the springs into the slots in lamination #2 to be sure that they have the proper angle. Glue them into place, making sure that they are 1/16" above the bottom of lamination #2 (Figure 4, front view). This clearance will prevent the springs from rubbing on lamination #3 when the key is turned.

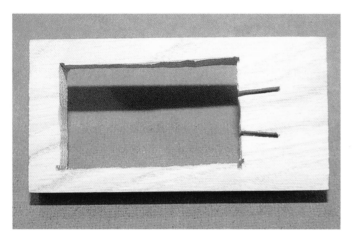

Lamination #2 ready for springs.

Lamination #2 with springs installed.

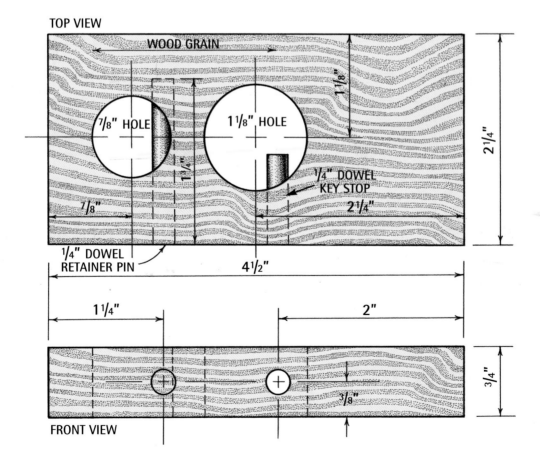

Figure 5. Lamination #3. Scale = full-size.

STEP 11

As before, lay out and mark the location of all holes before beginning to drill. I recommend that you drill the 1/4" holes in the side before drilling the 7/8" shackle hole. This will prevent the drill from deflecting when it hits the shackle hole. The shackle hole is drilled out next with a 7/8" wood bit all the way through the block. This hole is oversized to prevent the shackle from binding when it is moved either up and down or turned around when the lock is unlocked and open. Drill the 1-1/8" keyway hole all the way through the block. Glue the 1/4" x 15/16" key stop dowel (Figure 5) into place, making sure some glue gets into the hole with the dowel. Do not drive the dowel in too far or it will block the keyway, making it difficult or impossible to insert the key into the lock (Figure 5, top view).

Note that if you have a 1/4" plug cutter, you may want to recess this dowel 1/4" to make room for a wood plug made of the same wood as lamination #3. If you recess the keyway dowel, you will also want to recess the shackle retainer dowel, so make more than one plug for the 1/4" holes. The retainer dowel will be installed later, just before the lock is ready for finish.

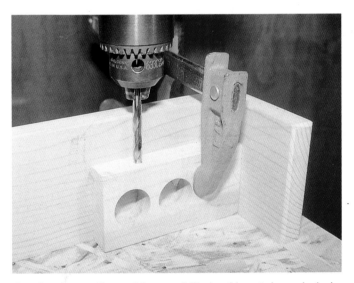

Lamination #3 in position to drill shackle retainer pin hole.

Lamination #3 showing key stop dowel.

STEP 12

Only the top of lamination #4 is shown in Figure 6 because all the holes go all the way through the workpiece. This lamination is the one that prevents the key from turning unless it is inserted all the way into the lock.

If you have not moved the drilling platform, drill the 3/4" shackle hole. If the platform has been moved, repeat step #2.

STEP 13

As before, find the exact center of the lamination. Lay out the keyhole location, and drill a 3/4" hole all the way through.

STEP 14

After you have drilled the two 3/4" holes at their proper locations, cut the two keyhole extensions to the right and left of the keyway hole. If you like, you can use a drill or a small pointed saw. These notches should be very close to 1/4" wide and make the keyhole 1-1/8" total width. If these notches are bigger, the key may be very loose and sloppy in the keyway. If the notches are too small, you will possibly have to shave or sand the key down to make it fit. Once you make this keyway hole, the key, which we will make a little later, will have to be made to fit.

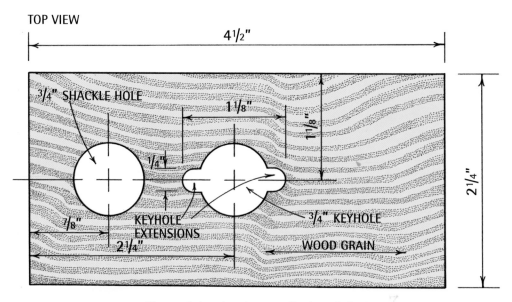

Figure 6. Lamination #4. Scale = full-size.

Lamination #4 Ready to Glue.

STEP 15

Drill the 7/8" shackle hole exactly 3/8" deep from the top of lamination #5. Lay out the exact center of the lamination. Then drill the 1-1/2" keyway hole exactly 3/8" deep, making sure it is in the exact center of the piece. Now turn the piece over and drill the 1-3/4" hole 3/8" deep through to the 1-1/2" hole (Figure 7, front). It is very important that the hole is centered and has the step all the way around. This is where the key slot insert will turn with the key.

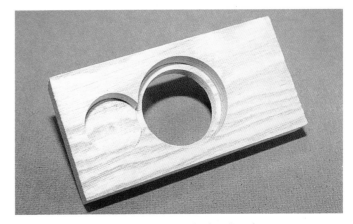

Cutout for key insert in lamination #5.

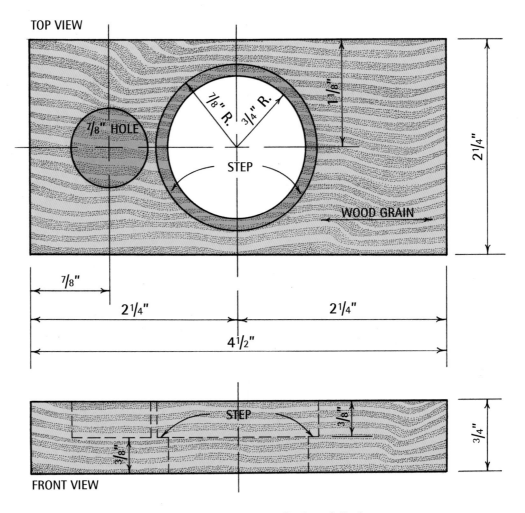

Figure 7. Lamination #5. Scale = full-size.

Key insert.

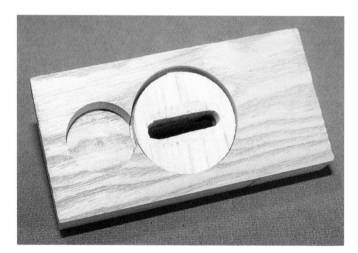

Lamination #5 with key insert in place.

STEP 16

We will now make the key insert.

Please note in Figure 8 that dimensions are the finish size. Pieces should be made a little oversized so they can be worked down to fit the insert hole in lamination #5.

Start with 3/8" thick wood to make the two respective pieces. The largest piece on the insert goes on the inside of the lock. It can be made of pine or another wood that is easy to cut and sand to shape. The smaller piece goes to the outside or bottom of the lock. Make this piece with whatever wood you like for appearance. Both of these pieces should be sanded down in size so that they turn freely with a little room to spare in case the wood expands or shrinks. The wood grain of the exterior piece should run in the same direction as the keyhole. When the two pieces are glued together, run the grains at 90° to each other to give strength to the insert. Now glue the two pieces together.

When the glue is dry on the key insert, carefully lay out the keyhole. Drill a 1/4" hole at each end of the key slot and two or three holes in between. Keep the holes in a straight line. I use a 3/8" chisel to carefully cut out and trim the rest of the slot. You may want to use a rasp or file to smooth out the keyhole.

Slip the insert into the recess in lamination #5 for a final fitting. Work down both the inside and the outside so that they are recessed just a little below the surface. Allow enough room for a little play (1/16") on the inside and enough on the outside so that when sanding down the lock body after gluing, you will not hit the insert.

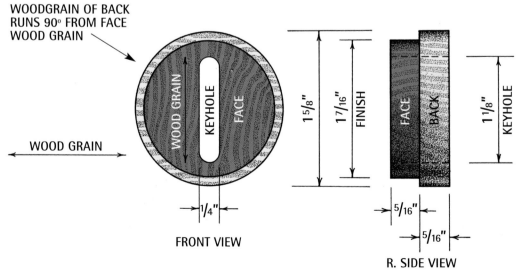

Figure 8. Key insert.

STEP 17

Select a piece of straight-grained hardwood for the key blank. I prefer ash or oak, but other hardwoods will work. Make a pattern from Figure 9 by tracing it onto a piece of paper. Try to be very accurate—check all measurements.

After cutting the blank 1/4" thick, 2" wide, and 5-1/2" long, lay carbon paper on the blank and transfer the pattern to the wood. Be very careful not to move the tracing while doing this. Cut out the key very carefully along the lines. The entire key is a little oversized at this time. Start out by sanding the flat sides so that the key will go into the key insert (Figure 8). Work carefully to round over all the edges until the key goes all the way into the insert. Dimension A in Figure 9 is the working part of the key. Do not cut this part of the key down very far. It will be finished after the lock body is glued together, which is the next step.

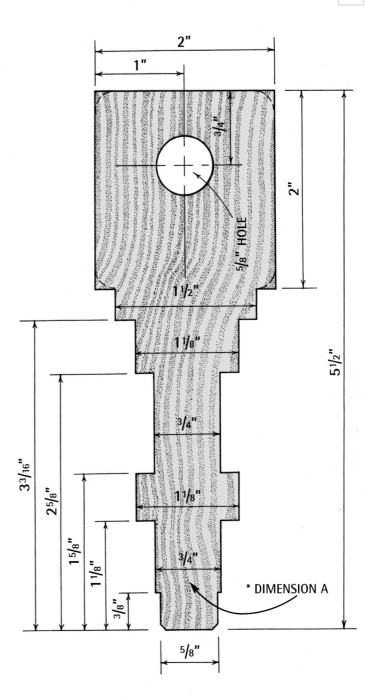

Figure 9. The key. Scale = full-size.

STEP 18

Stack all five laminations together in order (#1 is at the top). Don't forget the key insert in lamination #5. Line up all the pieces carefully and clamp them together so that you can try the key in the keyway. Pick up the lock and insert the key. While looking into the shackle hole in the top of the lock, slowly turn the key clockwise. The key should start to turn but don't force it. You'll see the locking springs start to move farther apart. Start to file or shave a little wood off of the key at dimension A in Figure 9. Take the same amount off each side of the key. Keep working this area down until the key is turned crossways to the stop, about 90°, and the springs are opened beyond the shackle hole. You can wait to do the final fitting until after the pieces of the lock body are glued together.

STEP 19

A small bead of glue just inside the edge will work best. You do not want glue running into the lock. Take special care gluing lamination #5 so that no glue gets into the recess around the key insert. If you get glue on the insert, your lock will not work. Hand-press the pieces together and let the glue set a couple of minutes, then clamp securely, making sure the laminations stayed in place and did not shift when pressure was applied. A bench vise is the best way to clamp the pieces together.

The lock body should look like the one pictured in Figure 1.

STEP 20

The shackle is probably the most difficult part of the lock to make. Select a piece of straight-grained wood that is 3/4" thick, 3-1/2" wide, and approximately 10" long. White pine is the easiest to work with but is not very strong. I recommend a good hardwood for the shackle, but it will be somewhat harder to work with. Remember to proceed carefully, as the shackle hole is exactly 3/4" in diameter. The final shackle will be approximately 1/16" smaller than the hole. It must move up and down as well as turn 360° freely.

Very carefully lay out the shackle outline on the wood to make a pattern. The notching will be done after the shackle is rounded and fitted into the lock. The final width of the shackle must be just a little less than the distance across the shackle holes in lamination #1 (probably a total width of 3-7/16").

The height of the shackle can be varied if you like. This will only affect how the lock looks, not how it works. May I suggest that you make the shackle ends 2" or 3" longer than you want the finished shackle? The reason for this is that you can leave the extra length square so that you will be able to clamp it down, making it easier to hold while rounding over.

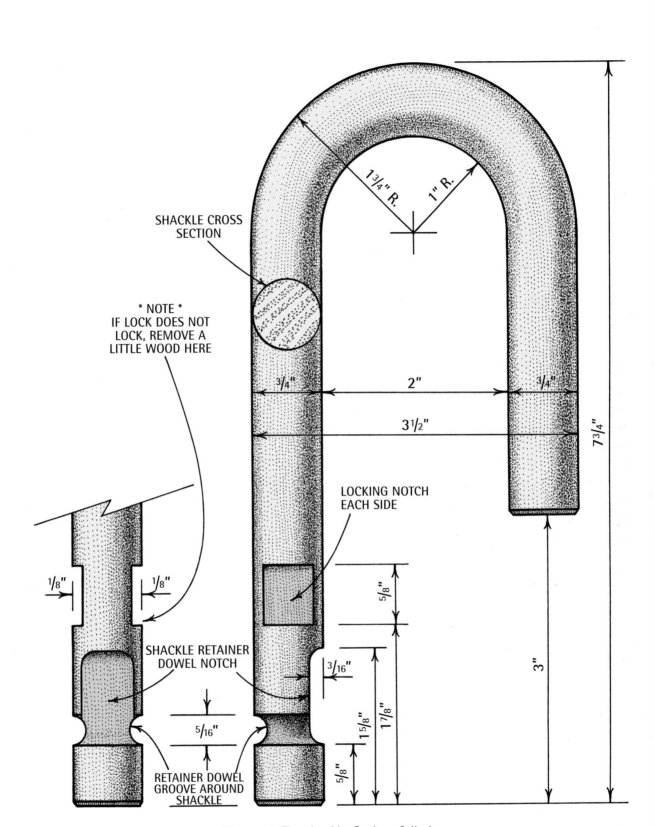

SHACKLE CROSS
SECTION

1¾" R.   1" R.

* NOTE *
IF LOCK DOES NOT
LOCK, REMOVE A
LITTLE WOOD HERE

¾"   2"   ¾"

3½"

7¾"

LOCKING NOTCH
EACH SIDE

⅛"   ⅛"

5/8"

SHACKLE RETAINER
DOWEL NOTCH

3/16"

3"

1 5/8"

1 7/8"

5/16"

5/8"

RETAINER DOWEL
GROOVE AROUND
SHACKLE

Figure 10. The shackle. Scale = full-size.

STEP 21

After cutting out the shackle, sand off the saw marks, and sand all surfaces so that the 3/4" thickness is now 1/32" undersized. This will help when the final fitting is done. If you have a router and a 3/8" roundover bit, rounding over will be much easier. Be very careful and take two or three passes to round over the shackle. Then remove the extra length from the shackle. This will allow you to finish both rounding over and sanding to fit the shackle holes. When you get to this point, you will need to have fitted the key to the lock so that you can spread the locking springs, allowing the shackle to enter the lock. Make sure both ends of the shackle hit the bottom of their holes.

STEP 22

When you are finished sanding the shackle, lay out the shackle retainer dowel groove—it goes all the way around the shackle 5/8" from the bottom (Figure 10). This notch can be made square instead of round if you prefer. Cut or carve this groove approximately 3/16" deep and 5/16" wide. Find a 1/4" x 3" dowel that will just slip into the retainer dowel hole in the lock body. You may have to sand down the dowel a little.

Now insert the shackle partway until the dowel goes into the hole all the way. If the dowel hits the shackle or rubs on it when the shackle is turned, remove more from the groove until it rotates freely.

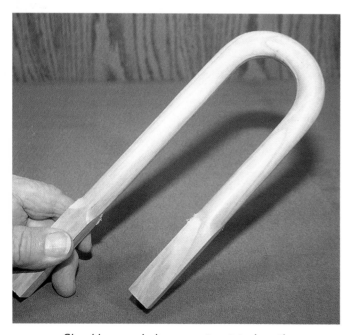

Shackle rounded over, not cut to length.

STEP 23

Lay out the shackle retainer dowel notch just above the groove. This notch is cut out to the same depth as the groove. If the shackle moves freely up and down and rotates 360° without binding, mark and cut the two locking notches on the sides of the shackle.

You have now come to the place where you have put quite a few hours into this project. At this point, you probably know that the lock works, but assemble it anyway and insert the dowel retainer pin temporarily—work the lock over and over, making sure it works to your satisfaction. If the lock does not snap and lock when closed, you probably need to cut just a little more out of the bottom of the two locking notches (see the note in Figure 10). Do one notch at a time until there is a little extra play up and down when locked.

Remove the shackle, and lay it aside. If you have not yet sanded down the lock body, do so now.

STEP 24

It's easiest to sand the lock body with a belt sander, but you can also do it by hand. Start with coarse sandpaper and proceed to 220 grit for the final sanding. I use a router and a 5/16" roundover bit to round all the corners of the lock body. If you're using a router, take two or three passes to eliminate grain tear-out. Also be careful not to run the bearing race of the router bit into the keyhole, or you will make a notch in the lock.

If you are rounding the corners by hand, use a hand plane or rasp and file followed by sanding.

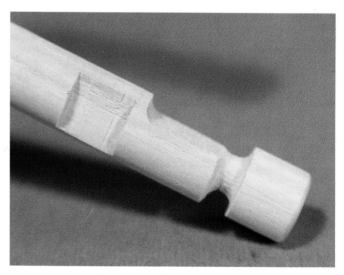

Shackle notched and ready to finish.

STEP 25

Insert the shackle and cut the retainer dowel pin to length (1/4" below the surface if you are going to use a wood plug in the hole). Put a bead of glue on the end of the dowel and insert it all the way into the hole. Glue the plugs into the holes, letting them stick up a little above the surface. When dry, cut or sand them off flush with the surface. Check all surfaces and sand all marks and scratches in preparation for applying the finish. This is the most important step in making a "showpiece" and not just a wooden lock. The time you spend on sanding now will pay off when you put the finish on.

As I stated earlier, I prefer polyurethane finish applied with a 2" foam brush. I prefer satin finish over gloss because it does not show imperfections as easily.

STEP 26

Clean the lock and key carefully with a vacuum and wipe them off with a tack cloth. Find a piece of wood about 3/16" thick by 1" by 8" to use as a holder. Unlock the lock and insert the holder in the keyway. Apply the finish to the shackle first, then to the lock body. Be careful not to leave runs in the finish. In addition, avoid getting finish in the space around the key insert in the bottom of the lock. I like to hang the lock on a nail until the finish is dry. If the key insert is stuck when the finish dries, use the holder to carefully break it free.

STEP 27

When dry, sand lightly along the grain using 400-grit or finer paper to remove any roughness or raised grain. Vacuum the surface and wipe it again with a tack cloth. Apply a second light coat of finish, covering all surfaces and not leaving any runs.

STEP 28

Put some paraffin or other wax on the part of the key that comes in contact with the locking spring (Figure 9, dimension A). Insert the key and turn it several times. The lock will work easily and smoothly.

I hope that you enjoyed making this wooden lock, and that you will proceed to make the other locks in this book. May I suggest that you sign and date the lock, so that it may become a family keepsake or a valued gift?

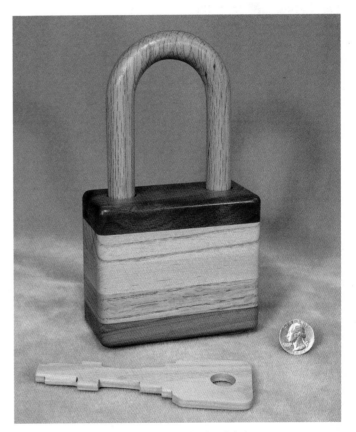

Finished warded lock with key.

Chapter Six
Three-Number Combination Lock

Making a combination lock is a bit more of a challenge than a warded lock. The dial and tumblers are the most difficult because they have to be made to very close specifications.

Start by selecting the wood. As with the warded lock, you may use pine if you like, but hardwoods are much more attractive and a bit stronger. My favorites are walnut for the lock body and dial knob, and ash or oak for the shackle and dial. I use one solid piece for the lock body, but you can glue pieces together if you wish. Please note that the lock body is 1-3/4" thick, 4-1/2" wide, and 4-1/2" high.

Do not cut the round bottom of the lock body until later on in the project.

Refer to Figure 2 in the previous chapter on making a drilling platform. If you do not have a drilling platform, make one. Check that the back and end pieces are square to the platform base. This will allow you to clamp the lock body in an upright position for boring the shackle holes, which will make drilling much easier. You can cut the bottom to shape after all the holes are drilled.

From this point on, I am going to presume that you have most of the following power tools: a table saw, drill press, band saw, belt sander, lathe, and router. It is possible to make this lock without these tools, but all of them are very helpful.

Drill all the holes in the following order, using Figure 11 for the hole locations.

STEP 1

Mark the retainer pinhole location (Figure 11) on the face of the lock body blank. Drill a 1/4" hole 1-1/2" deep from the front of the lock.

STEP 2

Lay out and drill the locking pinhole exactly 1-1/2" deep with a 1/2" Forstner bit, leaving 1/4" of wood at the back of the lock. Forstner bits are essential in making this lock.

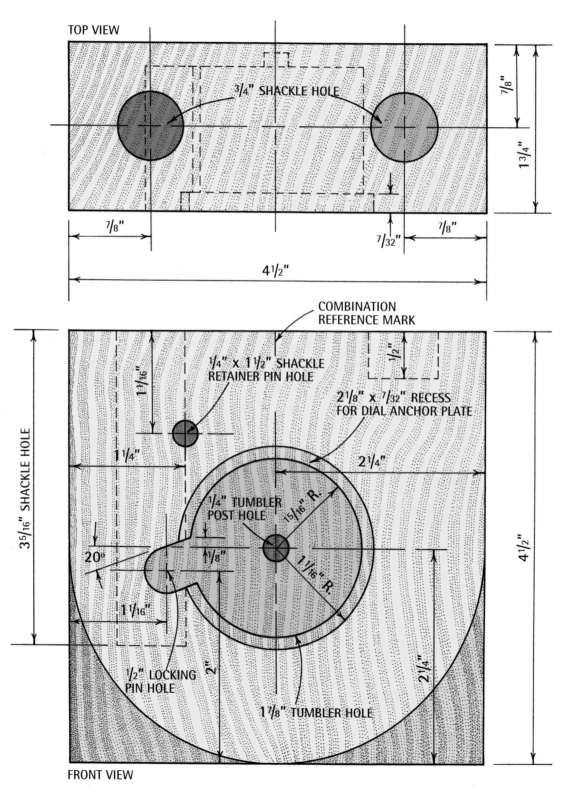

Figure 11. Lock body. Scale = full-size.

STEP 3

Lay out the two shackle holes on the top of the lock body (Figure 11). Clamp the lock body upright on the platform with the front toward you. Position the platform on the drill press and clamp securely into position.

Drill the long shackle hole using a 3/4" bit. Bore the hole exactly 3-5/16" into the lock body.

STEP 4

Move the workpiece or platform to line up and drill the other 3/4" shackle hole 1/2" deep.

STEP 5

Remove the lock body and lay out the tumbler posthole (as shown in Figure 11) in the exact center of the lock body.

STEP 6

Clamp the platform in place so that the drill hits right in the center of the lock face. Use a 2-1/8" Forstner bit to drill down 7/32" below the face of the lock for the anchor plate recess—make sure not to drill any deeper.

Note: Don't move the lock body. Remove the 2-1/8" bit.

STEP 7

Using a 1-7/8" Forstner bit, drill the tumbler hole in the same location down 1-1/2" from the face of the lock. This will leave 1/4" of wood in the back of the lock. This hole must be the same depth as the 1/2" locking pinhole in Step 2.

STEP 8

Do not move the lock body. Change to a 1/4" Forstner bit or possibly a brad point bit to bore the tumbler posthole. Set the depth of the drill so that you will leave about 3/32" at the bottom of the hole. Otherwise, you will drill through the back of the lock.

STEP 9

If you like, you can leave the lock body square-shaped. However, the round bottom is the shape of some real combination locks. If you make the bottom round, use a 2-1/4" radius not more than 2-1/4" from the bottom of the lock body. Notice in Figure 11 that the bottom of the long shackle hole is very close to the outside of the lock body when using the round bottom shape.

Lock body clamped to drilling platform, drilling shackle hole.

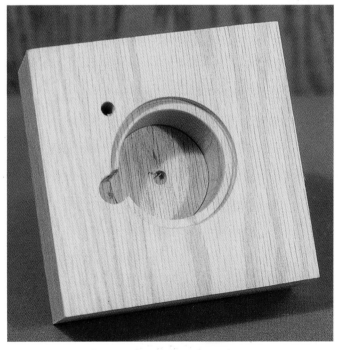

Recess for dial anchor plate.

STEP 10

Look again at Figure 11. The locking pinhole must be cut out at the angle shown into the tumbler hole. Note that the top of the slot is 1/8" above the lock centerline. Using a 3/8" chisel, cut out this slot very carefully so that a 1/2" dowel will roll in and out freely but not with a lot of extra room. The final fitting will be done later—when you are working on the tumblers and the shackle or at final assembly.

STEP 11

Prepare the lock for rounding the edges by first sanding all sides. A note of caution here: Do not sand the back of the lock more than absolutely necessary, as there is only from 1/16" to 3/32" of wood at the center where the tumbler post hole is located. If you should sand into this hole, it will not affect the lock other than the tumbler post dowel will show there.

STEP 12

I use a 3/16" radius roundover bit in my router for rounding all lock corners. If you can, clamp your router in a vise or use a router table; it will make the job much easier and safer.

STEP 13

Using the dimensions in Figure 12, lay out the shackle on a piece of straight-grained wood measuring 3/4" by 3-1/2" wide, and 10" long. Measure the width of the shackle across the holes you have drilled in the lock body, and adjust your layout of the shackle to fit, if necessary.

STEP 14

The height of the shackle can be made differently if you like. This will only affect how the lock looks and not how it works. May I suggest that you make the shackle ends 2" or 3" longer than you want the finished shackle? Leaving the extra length square allows you to clamp down the wood, making rounding over easier.

After cutting out the shackle, sand off the saw marks and sand down all surfaces so that the 3/4" thickness is now 1/32" undersized. This will help when the final fitting is done. If you have a router and a 3/8" roundover bit, rounding over will be much easier. Be very careful and take two or three passes to round the shackle over. After you're done, remove the extra length from the shackle to allow you to finish rounding over and sanding down to fit into the shackle holes. The shackle should be worked down so that it slides into the lock body and also freely turns 360° when pulled up about 3/4." Make sure the shackle hits the bottom of both holes when inserted.

STEP 15

Refer to Figure 12 and lay out the retainer dowel groove 1-9/16" from the bottom. You can carve, file, or saw this groove. As you work it down, keep testing the fit by inserting the shackle and slipping a 1/4" dowel temporarily into the retainer pinhole.

STEP 16

When the shackle pivots freely with the dowel inserted, lay out the retainer dowel notch and saw or carve it to the same depth as the groove around the shackle.

STEP 17

Lay out the locking pin notch by sliding the shackle all the way into the lock; with a sharp pencil, mark the shackle through the locking pinhole. Now carefully saw or carve the notch to fit the locking pinhole. Roll a piece of 1/2" dowel in and out of the notch. If the dowel does not roll freely, carve a little more out of the locking pinhole and/or enlarge the shackle notch. Do not remove too much wood, just enough for easy movement of the locking pin.

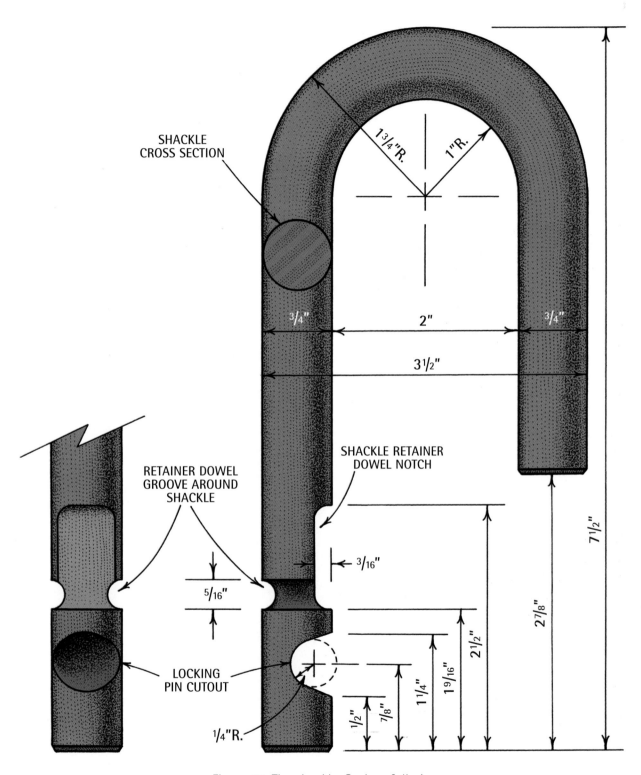

SHACKLE
CROSS SECTION

1³/₄"R.

1"R.

³/₄"

2"

³/₄"

3¹/₂"

SHACKLE RETAINER
DOWEL NOTCH

RETAINER DOWEL
GROOVE AROUND
SHACKLE

³/₁₆"

5/₁₆"

7¹/₂"

2⁷/₈"

2¹/₂"

1⁹/₁₆"

1¹/₄"

7/₈"

1/₂"

LOCKING
PIN CUTOUT

¹/₄"R.

Figure 12. The shackle. Scale = full-size.

STEP 18

I prefer to make the dial from the same kind of wood that the shackle is made of. Cut a piece of wood 3/8" thick, and 3-3/4" square (Figure 13). Make the knob of the same kind of wood as that of the lock body.

Saw the dial round as in Figure 13. Saw the knob from 3/4" wood approximately 1-1/2" in diameter. Glue the knob in the exact center of the dial. After the glue is dry, fasten the dial exactly in the center of a small lathe faceplate. Carefully turn down the dial and knob. The final dial should be 3-1/2" to 3-3/4" in diameter. Round the edges on the face to your liking, and sand to at least 220-grit sandpaper to remove all scratches.

STEP 19

Remove the dial from the faceplate and lay out the small indicator marks around the rim of the dial every 45° as in Figure 13. I use a wood burner to do this but you can carve a little notch or paint the marks on the dial if you like.

Next you must put on the numbers. Again, I use a wood burner, but you can carve or paint them. You may want to use a number template, if you have one available, to help with layout.

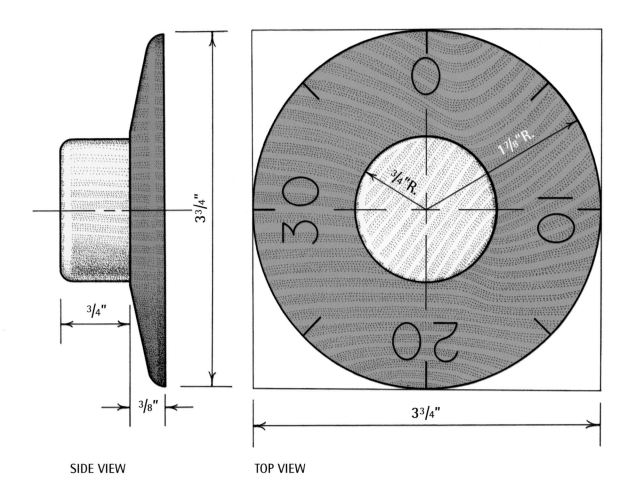

SIDE VIEW   TOP VIEW

Figure 13. The dial. Scale = full-size.

STEP 20

Find the exact center on the back of the dial. Using a 1/4"
drill in the drill press, drill 7/8" into the dial and knob.

Note: This hole in the dial must be perpendicular to the
back of the dial. Lay the dial aside with the lock body and
shackle for now.

STEP 21

To make the dial anchor plate, saw a round disk out of
1/4" plywood. Drill a 1/4" hole in the exact center.

If the anchor plate will not slip into the recess in the lock
face (Figure 11), sand all around the outside edge of the
anchor plate until it goes into the recess without forcing.
The anchor plate should stick up about 1/16" above the
face of the lock when lying in the recess.

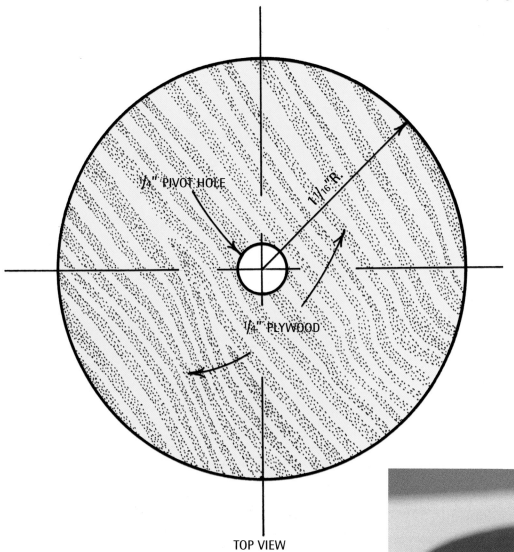

TOP VIEW

Figure 14. Dial anchor plate.

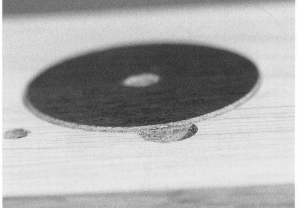

Anchor plate projects 1/16" above lock face.

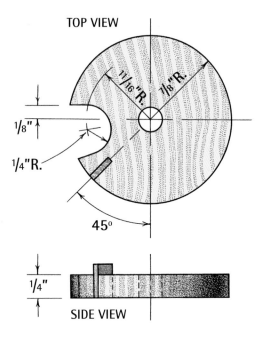

TOP VIEW

$1^{1}/_{16}$"R.

$^{7}/_{8}$"R.

$^{1}/_{8}$"

$^{1}/_{4}$"R.

45°

$^{1}/_{4}$"

SIDE VIEW

Figure 15. Tumbler #1. Scale = full-size.

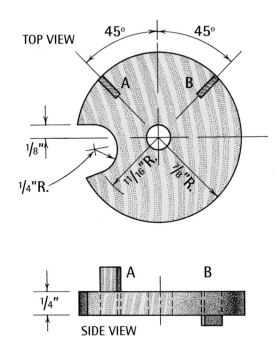

TOP VIEW

45°   45°

A   B

$^{1}/_{8}$"

$^{1}/_{4}$"R.

$1^{1}/_{16}$"R. $^{7}/_{8}$"R.

$^{1}/_{4}$"

A   B

SIDE VIEW

Figure 16. Tumbler #2. Scale = full-size.

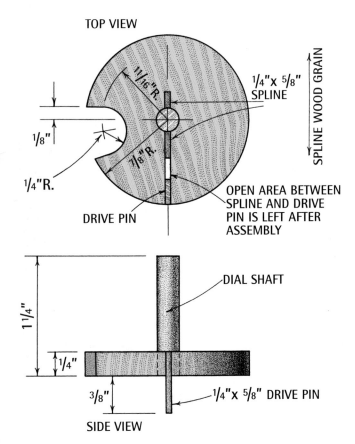

TOP VIEW

$1^{1}/_{16}$"R.

$^{1}/_{4}$"x $^{5}/_{8}$" SPLINE

SPLINE WOOD GRAIN

$^{1}/_{8}$"

$^{7}/_{8}$"R.

$^{1}/_{4}$"R.

DRIVE PIN

OPEN AREA BETWEEN SPLINE AND DRIVE PIN IS LEFT AFTER ASSEMBLY

DIAL SHAFT

$1^{1}/_{4}$"

$^{1}/_{4}$"

$^{3}/_{8}$"

$^{1}/_{4}$"x $^{5}/_{8}$" DRIVE PIN

SIDE VIEW

Figure 17. Tumbler #3 (drive tumbler). Scale = full-size.

Cutting drive pin notches.

STEP 22

On a piece of paper, carefully lay out a pattern from the drawing of the three tumblers in Figure 15, Figure 16, and Figure 17.

Transfer the patterns onto pieces of 1/4" plywood. If you can get plywood 7/32" thick, use it. The location of the locking pin notch and the drive pins must be exact or the combination will be changed.

Carefully cut out the tumblers. Mark the number of the tumbler and the top of each tumbler.

STEP 23

Drill the pivot hole with a 1/4" drill exactly in the center of each tumbler.

STEP 24

Saw the drive pin notches on a band saw. One cut approximately 1/16" wide should be enough.

When sawing the drive pin notch in tumbler #3 (Figure 17), saw in a straight line 1/8" beyond the pivot hole in the center.

STEP 25

Next cut the locking pin notch in each tumbler using a scroll saw or a band saw with a 1/8" blade.

STEP 26

Pick a piece of straight-, fine-grained ash or hickory (my favorite), and saw or sand down a spline to fit the cuts in the tumblers, 1/16" thick and 1/4" wide. You only need enough to make five pieces approximately 1/2" long, so make 5" or 6" of spline this size. I use sharp tin snips to cut the pieces to length as needed, but you can use a knife or fine-toothed saw.

STEP 27

Start with tumbler #1 (Figure 15). Cut a 1/2" piece of spline, and glue it flush with the underside and the outside edge into the notch in tumbler #1. Wipe the extra glue off and lay aside to dry.

STEP 28

Next cut two pieces of spline 1/2" long. Glue one into the notch lettered "A" in Figure 16, flush with the bottom and outside edge. Glue the other into the notch lettered "B" in Figure 16, flush with the top and the outside edge. Wipe extra glue off and set aside to dry.

Finished #1 tumbler.

Finished #2 tumbler.

Finished tumbler #3 .

Back of combination dial with reference mark shown.

STEP 29

Now cut a piece of 1/4" dowel 1-1/4" long for the dial shaft (Figure 17). Using the same saw that you used to cut the drive pin notches, make a 1/4" deep cut exactly centered into one end of the dial shaft. Cut a piece of spline about 5/8" long and glue it into the notch that you just cut in the dial shaft. Let only 1/8" of the spline stick out from one side and the rest out the other side. Cover the spline and a little of the shaft with glue and insert into the top of Tumbler #3. Make sure that the shaft is exactly perpendicular to the tumbler face and flush with the underside. Place the tumbler over the edge of a table or board and roll back and forth with your finger to see if the tumbler wobbles. If it does, straighten the shaft. If it is not straight, the dial will wobble when the lock is finished. Remove all extra glue from the tumbler.

Cut another piece of spline 5/8" long and glue it into the notch, flush with the top of the tumbler. Remove all extra glue and set the assembly aside to dry.

You are now ready to "make or break" your project, as we say.

I cannot stress too much the sanding process in preparation for applying the finish. Remember, always sand with the wood grain.

STEP 30

Sand the lock body on all outside surfaces, and sand the shackle holes just enough to take off the sharp corner. Sand the shackle all over, at least the portion that shows when the lock is open. Round over both ends of the shackle just a little. This will help it slide in the holes as well as enhance appearance. Next check the dial. Are all marks and numbers done to your satisfaction? Check all three tumblers, removing any slivers, beads of glue, and rough places.

STEP 31

Go back to the lock body (Figure 11). You have one final job to do. Measure across the face to find the center, 5/16" below the top of the lock. This spot is where you must put a reference mark for dialing the combination numbers.

I burn a 1/4" long vertical mark. You may want to carve a small groove or paint a mark. You can even drill a 1/8" hole and glue a wood plug into it. Just keep it narrow for accurate combination dialing.

Step 32

Now that all the hard work is done, let's apply the finish. First you must think of where to put the lock while the finish dries. I suggest clamping a 1/2" dowel in a vise. Let it stick up 5" or 6" above the vise so that you can slip the lock body down over it into the shackle hole.

I use three or four fingers stuck into the tumbler hole to hold the lock body while applying the finish. It is easier to apply finish to the top and the front of the lock before putting your fingers into the hole. Now you can turn the lock around easily to finish the job. Check to see if there are any runs in the finish.

Next drive a nail in a ceiling joist or somewhere that will not hurt anything for a place to hang the shackle. Hold the shackle by the long notched end and apply the finish. It is not necessary to apply finish farther than to the notches.

Drive a finish nail part way into a piece of board for a place to put the dial after applying the finish. When all the finish is dry, sand lightly with very fine sandpaper to remove any rough places or raised grain. Vacuum off all pieces and wipe with a tack cloth.

Step 33

Apply a second light coat of finish. The finishing should be done now, but if you like, you can repeat the last step. Let the finish dry completely before beginning final assembly.

Step 34

Find a 1/4" dowel that will just go into the tumbler posthole (Figure 11). Cut a piece 1-1/8" long and put some glue on the end. Insert it into the posthole and make sure it is all the way in and that some glue squeezes out. Wipe away any excess glue and make sure the post is perpendicular to the bottom of the tumbler hole.

Now take tumbler #3, and try inserting the dowel into the hole in the back of the dial. We want it to just slip in, so don't force it into the hole. Either sand the dowel if it is tight or drill out the hole a little with a 17/64" drill.

Take the anchor plate (Figure 14), and try to slide it onto the dial shaft (Figure 17). The anchor plate must spin freely on the dial shaft.

Put a mark on the backside of the dial exactly across from the #20 indicator mark on the dial face. This mark tells what the combination is (Figure 18).

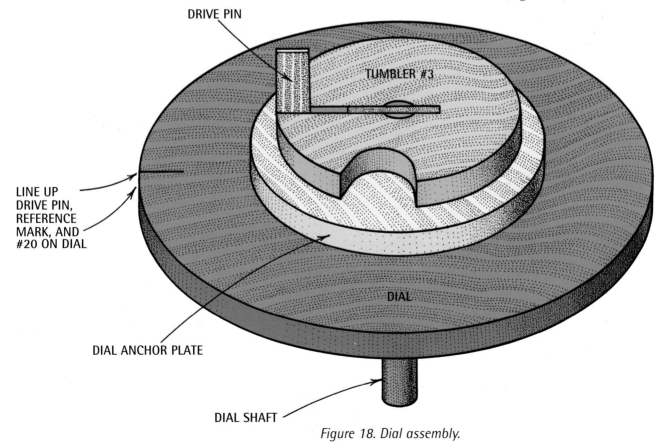

Figure 18. Dial assembly.

STEP 35

Dry-fit the anchor plate on the shaft of tumbler #3, and insert it into the hole in the dial. It must go all the way in. Remove it from the dial and read the gluing instructions before proceeding.

Do not put glue on the dial shaft. Instead, put a little into the hole in the dial. With the anchor plate on the dial shaft, insert it into the dial, turning as you go. Back it out part way and then insert it again. All the while keep in mind that the drive pin or spline must line up with the reference mark you put on the dial back. The anchor plate must turn freely, but not be too loose or the dial will flop and wobble around.

Note: Do not allow glue to get between the anchor plate and the dial, or the lock won't work.

STEP 36

Cut two 3/4" square spacers of 1/8" plywood, and drill a 1/4" hole in the exact center (Figure 19).

STEP 37

Take tumbler #1 and try to slide it onto the tumbler post dowel (Figure 11).

The tumbler must spin freely on the post. Enlarge the hole until it spins. Cut the drive pin to 3/32" above the tumbler (Figure 15).

Now take one plywood spacer (Figure 19), and slide it down on top of tumbler #1. If the spacer is tight on the tumbler post, raise it just a little until tumbler #1 turns freely with no catching. If the spacer is not tight on the spindle, put a little glue around the post, raise the spacer about 1/8," and push it back down. Wipe off the excess glue and adjust so that the tumbler rotates freely. Let sit for a few minutes until the glue sets.

STEP 38

Try tumbler #2 in the same way as tumbler #1. Cut the drive pin on the bottom of the tumbler to 3/32" from the surface. Cut the drive pin on the top to 1/4" from the surface (Figure 16). Make sure tumbler #2 is turned right side up. Install the other spacer using the same procedure as before. Glue and let dry.

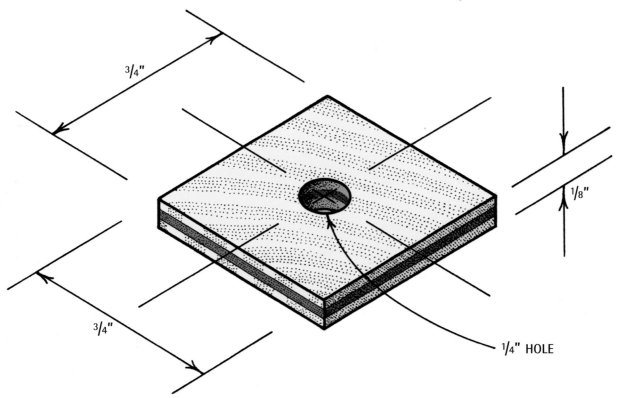

3/4"

3/4"

1/8"

1/4" HOLE

Figure 19. Spacer.

STEP 39

Cut a piece of 1/2" dowel 1-1/8" long. Sand the end of the dowel and round the corners over about 1/16."

Put the shackle into the lock; slip a 1/4" dowel into the retainer pinhole, and line up the notches in the tumblers at the locking notch.

Drop in the 1/2" locking pin and attempt to pull the shackle up.

As you pull up on the shackle, the locking pin should roll into the notches in the tumblers. If the shackle rises all the way to the top, try to rotate it 360º.

If the shackle binds or does not turn freely, you must find where it rubs or binds and remove a little wood to free it up. The most common problem spot is at the bottom end of the shackle. In this case, carve or sand all around the bottom of the shackle up about 1/2" or so. Take your time and proceed until the shackle works just right.

Turn the tumblers with the locking dowel in place and the lock is closed. They should turn without rubbing the locking pin. You may have to do a little adjusting and fitting.

STEP 40

Once all is working to your satisfaction, cut a 1/4" x 1-3/8" dowel from the dowel you used as a temporary retainer pin.

Put a bead of glue on the end of the dowel and push it all the way into the retainer pinhole. If the pin is a little below the face of the lock, put a little bead of glue in the hole on top of the dowel.

Photo 22. Tumblers lined up at locking notch.

Measuring length of drive pin from face of lock.

STEP 41

Line up the notches in the tumblers and open the lock. Now measure from the face of the lock down to the top of tumbler #2.

This should measure very close to 13/16". Now measure from the back of the dial. Using your measurement, mark the drive pin on the drive tumbler and cut 1/8" shorter than this mark.

Double-check your measurements before cutting. If you cut too much off you will have to replace the pin on tumbler #2, or the drive pin on the dial assembly.

Turn #0 on the dial to the combination reference mark and lay the dial assembly into its recess on the lock.

Hold the dial with your fingers, so it cannot fall. Hold the lock upright, and close the shackle.

Try to turn the dial. If the dial does not turn, just jiggle it a little. Don't force it. The dowel has to roll down the slope to lock. As soon as the dial turns, the lock is locked. Gently pull on the shackle to check.

Measuring length of drive pin from dial back.

STEP 42

The combination:

1. Turn the dial counter-clockwise three times to #5.

2. Turn the dial clockwise two times to #25.

3. Turn the dial counter-clockwise one time to #0.

Open the lock. It should open very easily. If not, remove the dial assembly to see if the notches in the tumblers are in the right position. If there is a problem, it will usually be in tumbler #2. Try the combination again. This time use the numbers 5-26-0. You may have to add or subtract one number at a time to any of the numbers. Each time you will remove the dial to check the position of the notches. Remember, the bottom tumbler #1 goes counter-clockwise, and the top tumbler #2 goes clockwise.

You can check the third number by reading the number on the dial when the lock is open.

You probably know now why I stressed accurate layout and cutting. A lot of different things can change the combination a little.

Once you have the combination, work the lock several times to be sure that it always works.

Now that the lock works to your satisfaction, open the shackle and leave it open. Remove the dial assembly, and run a small bead of glue around the ledge for the anchor plate, and lay in the dial assembly.

Try the lock one more time before the glue sets.

"Congratulations!" You have made something that will be a gift of love, and a family heirloom to be handed down to children and grandchildren.

Finished three-number combination lock.

Combination lock with woods from around the world.

Chapter Seven
Antique Lever Lock with Key

The history of the lever lock goes back several cen-
turies. Many styles and shapes were produced using a
variety of materials.

The first lever lock we will discuss and make is in the
shape of an old lock that I found on a fishing trip to
Canada in 1958. The water level of the lake we fished on
was 12 to 15 feet below normal, which exposed a lot of
extra land. We located an old lumberman's campsite,
and among the things we found was an old lever pad-
lock. The lock that we will make in this chapter is the
shape of that lock.

First of all, choose the wood to be used. Pine will make a
nice lock body and shackle, but remember that although
pine is easier to work with, it is not as strong or colorful
as some of the hardwoods. My all-time favorite is crotch
or curly grain walnut for the lock body and ash or oak for
the shackle, keyhole trim, and wood buttons. If you have
or can get them, some of the imported woods such as
padauk, lacewood, zebra wood, and purple heart are very
colorful but they are also much more expensive.

STEP 1

You need two pieces of wood for the front and back of the lock body. If you have a supplier of 3/8" or 1/2" thick lumber, it makes finding wood easier, but you still will probably not have much choice of wood. I resaw my own pieces on a band saw. This allows me to pick any piece of wood that I wish to use.

STEP 2

Using Figure 20, cut the two pieces for the front and back exactly to size (5-1/2" wide by 6" long). Lay out the keyhole and the location of the four 3/8" holes for the buttons on the face of the lock.

STEP 3

Mark all pivot points (6) for the layout of the lock body outline, and use a compass to draw the outline using radiuses as shown. Do not cut to shape now.

STEP 4

Use a drilling platform on your drill press (Figure 2, Chapter 5). Lay the face lamination smooth side down on the platform. Set up and drill the 1/2" keyhole in the face of the lock (Figure 20). After you drill the keyhole, don't move the platform.

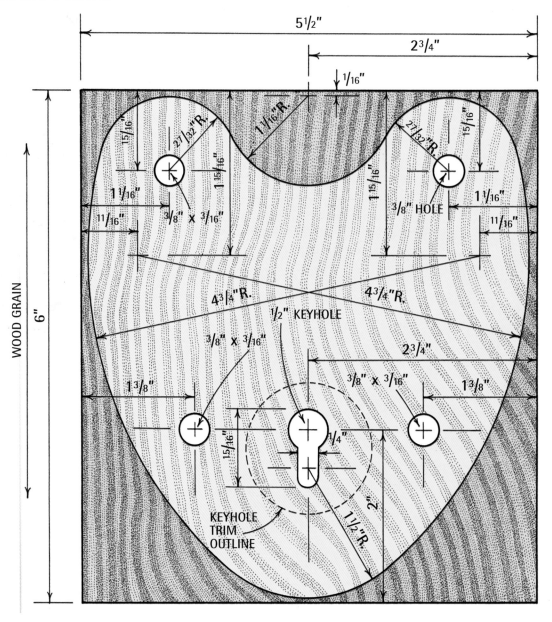

Figure 20. Lock face.

STEP 5

Replace the 1/2" drill with a 1/4" Forstner bit. Set the depth so the bit stops 3/32" from the platform. Now place the back of the lock on the platform. The smooth side of the back piece that will be inside the lock should be turned up. Drill the 1/4" hole in the back for the key pivot dowel. While you have the back of the lock in hand, lay out the lever pivot hole (Figure 21), and drill a 1/4" hole the same depth as the key pivot hole that you just drilled. Now lay the back aside, and return to the lock face piece.

STEP 6

Put a 3/8" drill in the drill press, and drill the four 3/16" deep holes for the wood buttons. The hole at the upper right—the shackle retainer hole—must be drilled through the face piece.

STEP 7

On the face piece, lay out the rest of the keyhole (Figure 20), if you have not done so already, and drill a 1/4" hole at the bottom of the keyway. Carefully saw or chisel out the remainder of the hole. After the lock is assembled you may have to do a little more fitting of the keyhole.

Lay the face piece on top of the back piece. Line up the sides and bottom and check to see if the key pivot hole is in the center of the keyhole. It should be.

Lay these two pieces aside until you glue the lock body together.

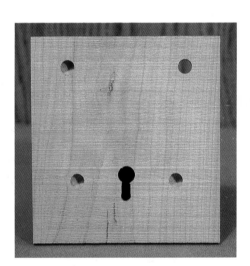

Face lamination with all holes bored out.

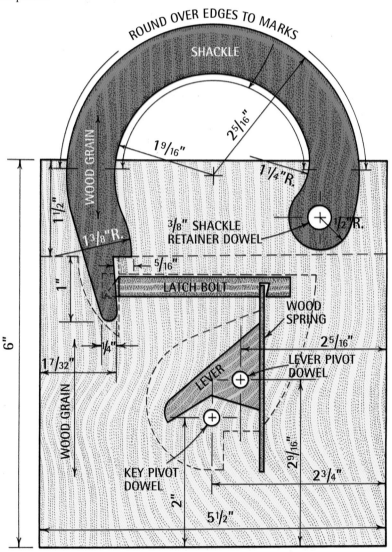

Figure 21. Lock back and interior parts.

Step 8

Pick out the piece of wood you want to use for the center lamination of the lock body. This can be the same kind of wood as the front and back or the same as the shackle. Either will look nice.

Use Figure 22 to lay out the center lamination. For accuracy, I suggest that you trace the pattern on a piece of paper and then transfer it to the wood with carbon paper. Saw out the piece very carefully with a band saw or scroll saw.

The size of this piece is very important. Pay close attention to the shackle notch, latch bolt slot, and spring slot.

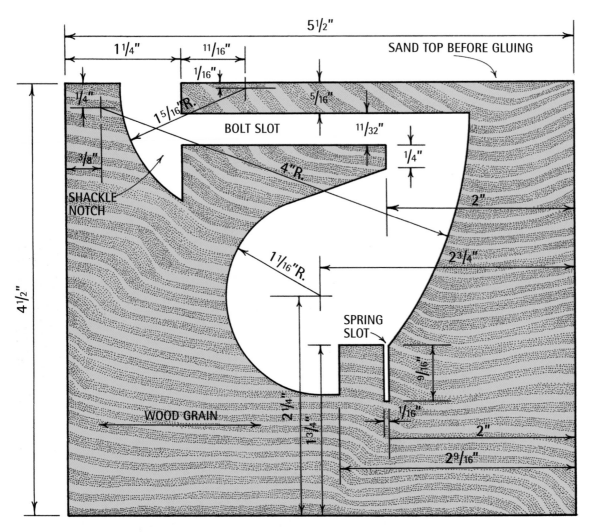

Figure 22. Body center lamination. Scale = full-size.

STEP 9

Make a wood spring of straight-grained ash or hickory (Figure 23).

Try the wood spring in the spring slot (Figure 22). Place a little glue on the end of the spring, or in the slot, and press the spring firmly into place. Center the spring in the slot. The top end of the spring should be about 3/16" from the top of the latch bolt slot (Figure 21 and photo at left below).

The spring should rest against the stop at the top with a little tension. This will make the lock close with a snap.

STEP 10

Cut a piece of 1/4" dowel 5/8" long and sand the end, rounding over the edges slightly. Put a bead of glue on the other end and tap the dowel into the key pivot hole (Figure 21).

STEP 11

Cut a piece of 1/4" dowel 7/8" long. Put a bead of glue on one end and tap into the lever pivot hole (Figure 21). Make sure both dowels are perpendicular to the back.

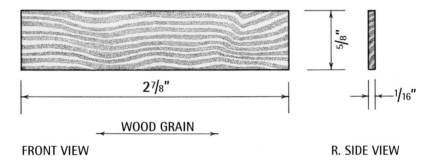

WOOD GRAIN

FRONT VIEW   R. SIDE VIEW

Figure 23. Wood spring. Scale = full-size.

Center lamination cutout with spring installed.

Back lamination with pivot dowels.

STEP 12

The latch bolt is made of straight-grained pine or any other good wood.

Note: In detail "A" of Figure 24, the notch is wider at the top of the cutout than at the bottom. This allows the end of the spring to move when the latch bolt is retracted. The notch opening should be just big enough for the latch spring to slip in.

Sand the latch bolt just enough to smooth the saw marks. The latch must move freely back and forth in the latch slot (Figure 22).

STEP 13

Carefully draw a pattern of the lever onto a piece of paper. Transfer it to a piece of 3/4" wood. Make sure the wood grain is as shown in Figure 25.

I like to drill the 1/4" hole for the pivot first. Be sure to center it as shown.

Cut out the side view first and then cut the notch. This notch is where the key comes in contact, so sand it smooth. Round all edges slightly with sandpaper.

Make sure the lever is 1/16" thinner than the center lamination.

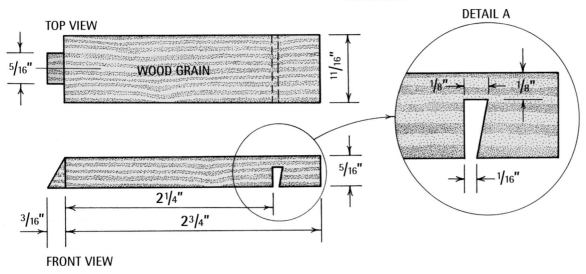

Figure 24. Latch bolt. Scale = full-size.

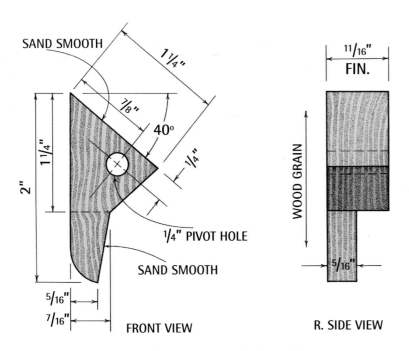

Figure 25. Lever. Scale = full-size.

STEP 14

Lay the back lamination on a flat surface. Place the center lamination even on the sides and bottom and on top of the back lamination. Lay the latch bolt into the latch groove. Now install the lever on the lever pivot. You may have to drill out the hole in the lever just a little to free it.

Line up the two laminations on the sides and bottom again. Clamp or hold firmly, and push the lever arm with your finger. If everything is lined up properly and does not bind, the latch bolt will retract, then spring back when released. If anything needs a little fitting to make it work, do it now.

STEP 15

Remove the latch and lever. Apply glue sparingly on the underside of the center lamination. Put a very small bead of glue on any portion of the lock near the latch bolt cutout. Keep in mind that if any glue gets on the latch, your lock will not work. I know, because it has happened to me, and the lock was ruined.

Place the center lamination on the back piece without sliding it around. If you slide the pieces, you may get glue on the latch bolt. Now put glue on top of the center lamination as you did on the backside. Carefully place the latch bolt and the lever in place. Lay the face or front of the lock carefully in place. Make sure that all three laminations are even on both sides and the bottom of the lock. Let set a couple of minutes. Clamp in a vise slowly, making sure that the pieces stay lined up perfectly. Use whatever clamping is needed to keep the edges tightly together. If you can, stick a finger or other object in the shackle hole and push on the latch bolt. If the bolt moves in all the way and springs back, you are done. If not, remove the clamps and pull the top lamination off quickly before the glue sets.

Check each piece to see what needs to be done to free the latch bolt. Repeat the gluing procedure.

Back and center laminations with all interior parts.

Glued lock body ready to saw out and sand to shape.

STEP 16

Referring back to Figure 21, draw a pattern for the shackle. Make sure to mark the center of the shackle retainer pinhole. Transfer the pattern onto the piece of 3/4" wood that you chose for the shackle, making sure the wood grain runs as shown in Figure 21. I recommend that you not cut a notch in the shackle for the latch bolt at this time.

Drill a 3/8" hole for the shackle retainer pin all the way through the shackle.

Sand the saw marks off with a drum or spindle sander. Smooth any uneven places so you have a nice even curve around the shackle.

On a belt sander, sand the sides nice and smooth, and sand down until the shackle slips into place between the ears on the lock top. There should be approximately 1/16" clearance. A little more clearance will not matter. Taper the sides at the latch end of the shackle as shown in Figure 26.

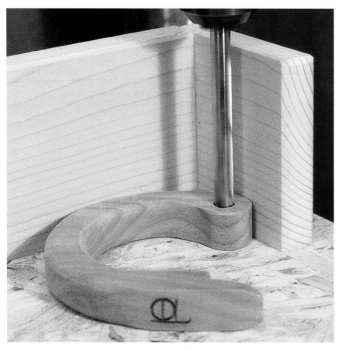

Drilling retainer pinhole in the shackle.

STEP 17

Drill a 1/2" recess into the shackle for the latch bolt, as shown in Figure 26, and cut out the end of the hole with a small chisel. Be careful not to split the end of the shackle or to cut completely through.

STEP 18

Refer to Figure 21 and mark where the router cuts stop on the edges of the shackle. Use a 3/16" roundover bit in the router to round the corners. You may use a 1/8" or 1/4" bit if you like.

STEP 19

Put a 3/8" drill in the drill press and set it so that it comes down to 1/8" from the platform. Place the lock body in position and drill through the shackle retainer hole down to the stop. This hole will hold the shackle retainer pin in place.

Cut a 2" long piece of 3/8" dowel to use for the shackle retainer pin. This dowel must turn freely in the hole in the shackle.

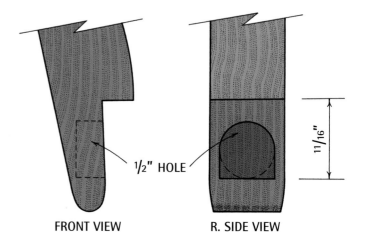

FRONT VIEW   R. SIDE VIEW

Figure 26. Shackle recess.

STEP 20

Saw a 3/16" piece of wood from the same kind of wood used for the shackle to measure 2" wide and 6" (or more) long.

Now trace the pattern from Figure 27 on a piece of paper, and transfer it to one end of the wood piece you just made.

Drill out the 1/2" hole and cut the key slot before cutting out the circle. Do not throw the rest of this wood away. We will use it to make the key.

Sand the keyhole trim piece smooth and round, then sand the keyhole and round the edges of the face side slightly.

STEP 21

Using the leftover piece of wood from the keyhole trim, use a compass to make a 1-3/4" circle on the 3/16" thick wood. Mark the center of the circle and bore the center hole with a 3/4" bit. Lay a piece of wood under your workpiece before drilling to keep from splintering the underside. Refer to Figure 28.

Cut another 3/16" thick piece of wood measuring 5/8" wide and 7/8" long. The wood grain should run in the 7/8" direction. We will call this piece the "bit." Sand the sides of this piece and the finger piece smooth.

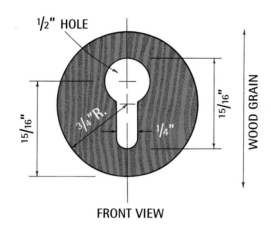

Figure 27. Keyhole trim. Scale = full-size.

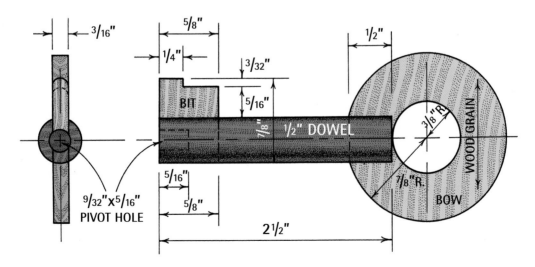

Figure 28. The key. Scale = full-size.

STEP 22

You may want to make a key jig to use on your band saw to hold the key shaft dowel while cutting the slot in each end (Figure 29).

You can use any piece of scrap wood for the base of the jig. Fasten two strips parallel, 3/8" apart, and high enough so that when the 1/2" dowel is laid in the groove it will not hit the base.

STEP 23

Cut a piece of 1/2" dowel 2-1/2" long for the key shaft. Make a straight pencil mark along one side of the key shaft dowel. Now make a mark 1/2" from one end and another mark 5/8" from the other end across this line.

Lay the key shaft in the jig with the long pencil mark at the center of the top.

Hold down firmly and make a saw cut beside the line. Stop at the cross mark 1/2" from the end. Keep making the cut wider until the finger piece just slips into the groove. Cut the slot in the exact center of the dowel.

Now make the 5/8" deep cut in the other end for the key bit. Make sure that the two cuts at either end of the dowel line up. If things do not come out right, make another dowel and try again.

Next glue the bit into the 5/8" notch in the key shaft. Make sure that glue is on all parts that come together. Let the glue set completely. We will come back to the key later.

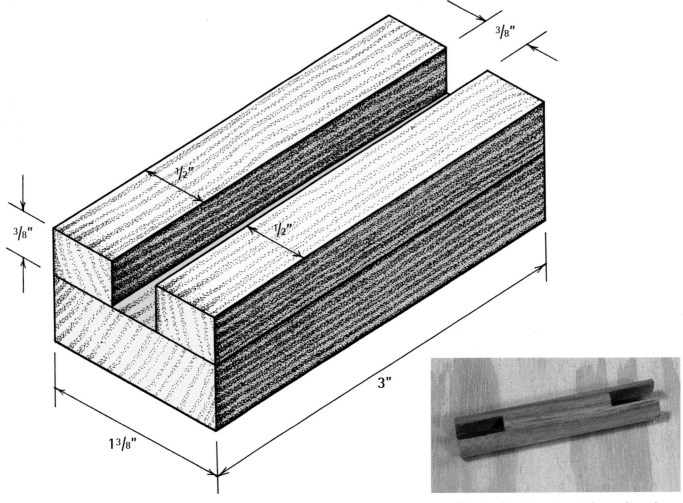

Figure 29. Key jig.

Key shaft with cutouts in each end.

STEP 24

Sand the front and back of the lock body smooth. Lay the pattern you made of Figure 21 on the lock body face. Using carbon paper, mark the heart-shaped outline onto the lock body. Make sure your pattern does not move. Check the outline on the lock to make sure it is centered. If everything looks right, saw the outline on the band saw or scroll saw.

Smooth all saw marks with a drum or spindle sander. Make all curves nice and even. This is the shape of your finished lock.

STEP 25

If the lock back and face are made of 3/8" thick wood, use a 1/4" roundover bit in your router to round over the front and back edges. Check to make sure the bearing on the cutter does not run off the underside of the piece as you rout the top curves. If it does, use a smaller roundover bit.

STEP 26

Go back to the key now (Figure 28). Using a 9/32" bit, drill a 5/16" deep hole in the bit end of the key shaft. This hole must be in the center. Drill slowly so the drill does not split out.

Turn the finger piece so the wood grain runs as shown and sand a flat place 1/2" long on one edge with the wood grain. This flat place fits the bottom of the slot in the key shaft. Place some glue in the slot at the end of the dowel shaft, and carefully press the finger piece into place. Wipe any excess glue off and let it dry.

When the glue is set, mark the lever notch on the key bit (Figure 28), and cut a little wood from the notch. Note that the key bit is rounded over in the end view of the key.

STEP 27

Try the key in the lock, but do not force it. You may have to file or carve the keyhole a little bigger for the key to fit.

When the key goes all the way in, it will turn. Again, do not force the key to turn. Your goal is to have the key turn clockwise about a half-turn, and stop against a stop that is built into the lever inside the lock.

Work carefully, removing wood from the lever notch (Figure 28). Each time you turn the key, look in the shackle hole and watch the latch bolt retract. Continue fitting the key until the latch draws back flush with the shackle hole when the key is turned to the stop.

Now install the shackle temporarily, and put the shackle retainer pin into place. Work the lock several times. Make sure the shackle does not bind or rub the sides. Sand and fit as needed to make it free. If the latch bolt does not snap into the shackle, remove the shackle and cut a little wood from the square end of the latch hole in the shackle until the lock works.

When the lock and key work properly, install the shackle and seat the retainer pin all the way in. Make a pencil mark at the lock face. Remove the pin and cut 3/16" shorter than the mark.

Remove the shackle pin and shackle.

Using chisel to enlarge locking notch.

STEP 28

Sand all exposed surfaces of the lock body, shackle, key, and keyhole trim. Sand with the grain of the wood. Keep sanding with finer sandpaper until you finish with 220 grit.

When all sanding is completed, take the keyhole trim piece and make sure the key will pass through it easily.

You can glue the keyhole trim on the lock face now if you want, but it is harder to keep the finish from making runs around it. If you put on all the finish before gluing the trim piece on, leave an area around the keyhole bare because glue will only stick to bare wood.

Now select four 3/8" wood buttons to be glued in the four holes in the lock face. I like to match the kind of wood used for the shackle and keyhole trim.

Clean all the wood with a vacuum cleaner and wipe off with a tack cloth.

Drive four nails into a joist or other handy place to hang the lock pieces to dry.

Start with the shackle. Hold it at the pivot hole and brush on the finish everywhere except where your fingers are. This will not show after assembly. Hang on a nail to dry.

The lock body should be finished from the top of the lock down. Note: Do not let any finish get into the shackle hole. If it gets on the latch bolt, the lock will probably be ruined because the bolt will not work. You can hold the lock with your fingers for most of the finish application. Then finish the job by inserting the key, and holding the lock by the key to finish the job. Check for runs in the finish, smooth out, and hang the lock on a nail.

Stick a piece of 1/4" dowel into the hole in the end of the key to hold it while putting on the finish.

The keyhole trim is finished only on the outside edge and the face, not on the back.

Put finish on the heads of the four buttons.

When the finish has dried, sand all surfaces lightly with very fine sandpaper. Vacuum the wood and wipe it down again with a tack cloth. Then apply the second coat of finish.

If you want to add a third coat of finish, repeat the finish application again.

STEP 29

When the finish is completely dried, put a small bead of glue on one end of the shackle retainer pin, position the shackle, and push the dowel all the way in. It should be 3/16" below the face of the lock. This leaves room for the wood button.

Make sure the shackle opens and closes properly.

Try the buttons in the holes. If they are too tight, use the point of a sharp knife to take just a little off the edge of the holes. Use a nail to spread a little glue around the edge of the holes and tap the buttons in tightly to the lock face.

Now spread a little glue on the keyhole trim, but not so much that it squeezes out around the edge. Place carefully over the keyhole, making sure it is straight.

This completes the antique lever lock.

I hope you enjoyed making the lock, and that you will also make the railroad switch lock in the following chapter.

Finished antique lever lock with key.

Chapter Eight
Railroad Switch Lock

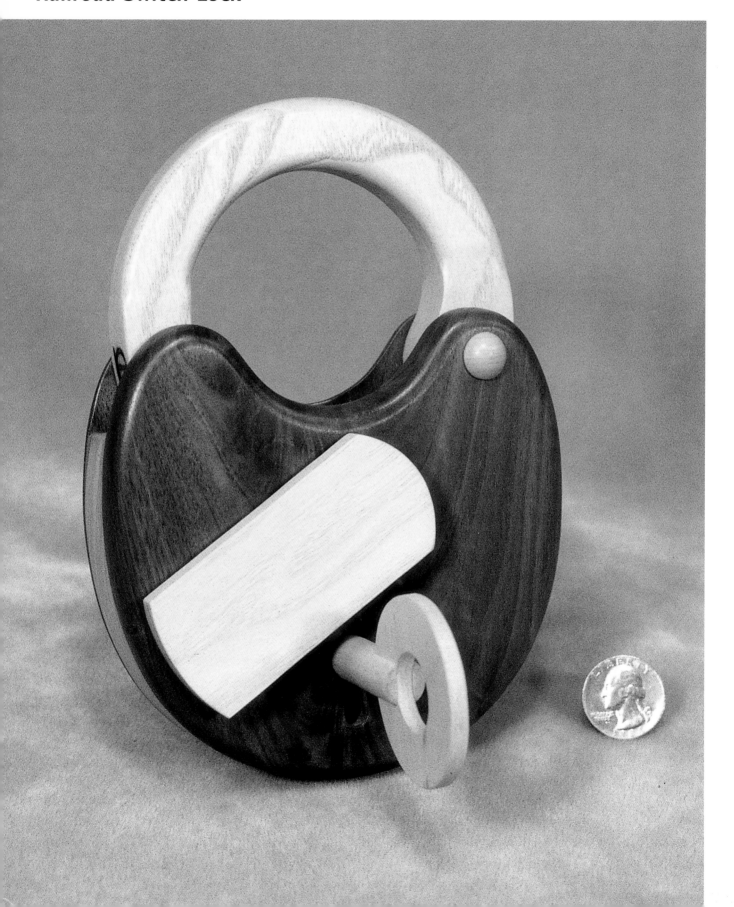

The railroad switch lock is a variation of the antique lever lock in the previous chapter. The shape and overall look of this lock resemble one that was patented in 1856. These locks were used extensively to lock the switches on the railroad tracks. Having a cover over the keyhole, the lock could always be opened in bad weather. This same type of lock is still manufactured today and, when it is made from metal, is used in high-security applications.

Begin by selecting the woods for the lock. You will need the following pieces:

1. Lock front: 3/8" thick, 5-1/2" wide, 5-1/2"long. The wood grain runs vertically.

2. Lock back: 3/8" thick, 5-1/2" wide, 5-1/2" long. The wood grain runs vertically.

3. Lock body center lamination: 3/4" thick, 4" wide, 5-1/2" long. The wood grain runs along the length.

4. Shackle: 3/4" thick, 4-3/4" wide, 4-3/4" long.

5. Keyhole cover: 1/4" thick, 1-1/2" wide, 3-1/2" long.

Pieces 1-3 should be the same kind of wood. Pieces 4 and 5, along with a 3/8" wood button, should be the same kind of wood. All other pieces will be made as needed.

STEP 1

Carefully trace over Figure 30, to make the pattern for this lock. It's essential that you transfer all the markings accurately, so take your time and work with caution.

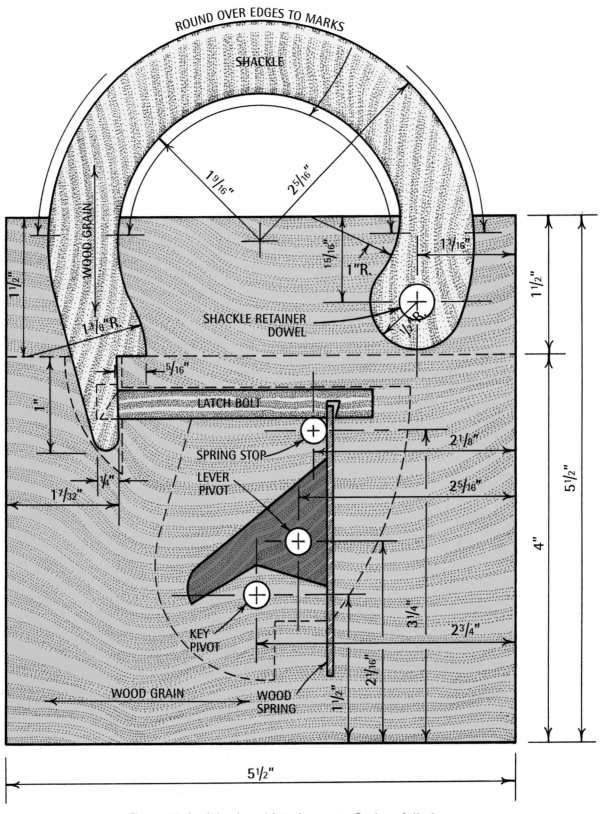

Figure 30. Lock back and interior parts. Scale = full-size.

STEP 2

Lay the back lamination of the lock body on a flat surface, smooth surface up. Orient the wood so the grain is vertical. Using carbon paper and your pattern, mark the center for the key pivot hole, the lever pivot, and the spring stop on the wood.

STEP 3

With a Forstner or brad point bit, drill 1/4" holes at all three locations. Set the drill to stop 1/8" short of breaking through the wood.

STEP 4

Reproduce Figure 31 on a paper pattern. Be accurate, marking all six pivot points for drawing the body outline with a compass. Also mark the center of the shackle retainer pin, the keyhole cover mount, and the keyhole.

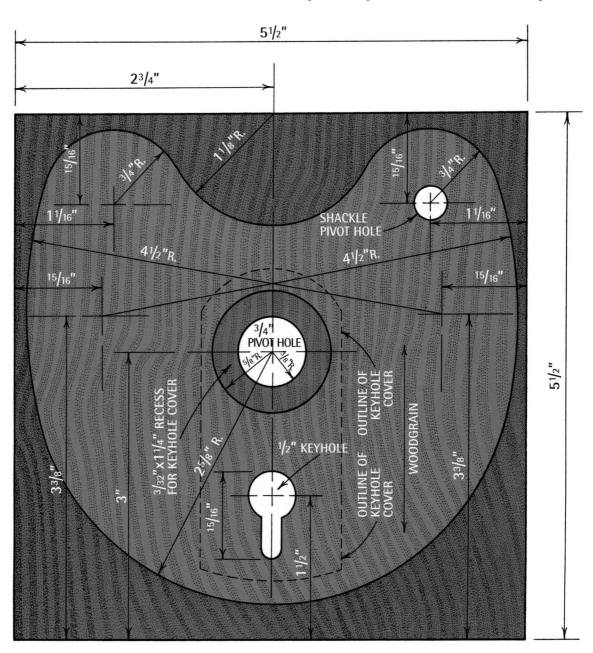

Figure 31. Lock face. Scale = full-size.

Step 5

Now turn the smooth side of the face lamination down. Using carbon paper, mark the center location of the 1-1/2" x 3/16" keyhole cover mounting hole, the shackle pinhole, and the keyhole.

Step 6

Use a 3/8" Forstner bit to drill the shackle pivot pinhole all the way through the face lamination.

Step 7

Now change to a 1-1/4" Forstner bit. Bore the keyhole cover recess hole exactly 3/16" deep into the face lamination.

Step 8

Change to a 3/4" bit and drill a hole all the way through the exact center of the 1-1/4" recess hole.

Step 9

Use a 1/2" drill to bore the keyhole, and use a 1/4" drill to drill out the bottom of the keyway. Then carefully cut out the remainder of the keyhole with a chisel or sharp knife.

Lock face with holes bored.

STEP 10

Now make a pattern of the center body lamination from Figure 32. Make certain the pattern is placed exactly right on the wood blank. Tape it in place and, using carbon paper, transfer the pattern to the workpiece.

Carefully saw out the center lamination with a band saw or scroll saw. Be extra careful while sawing the latch bolt slot, the spring slot, and the notch for the shackle.

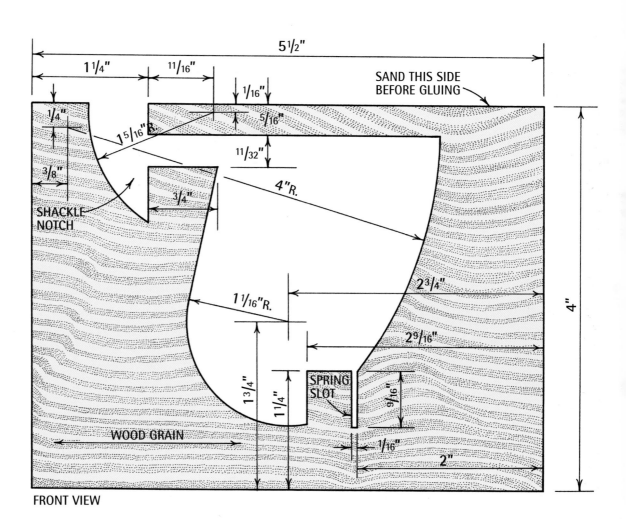

Figure 32. Body center lamination. Scale = full-size.

STEP 11

Go to the back lamination and cut one piece of 1/4" dowel 5/8" long. Slightly round over one end with sandpaper, put a bead of glue on the other end, and push it firmly into the key pivot hole. Remove the excess glue.

Cut two pieces of 1/4" dowel 7/8" long, and glue them into the lever pivot and spring stop holes. Make sure all dowels are perpendicular to the back. Wipe off any extra glue, and lay aside to dry.

STEP 12

Make a wood spring of straight-grained ash or hickory.

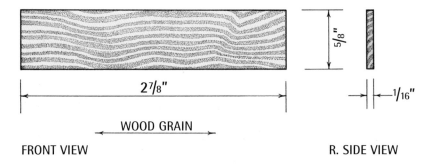

FRONT VIEW   R. SIDE VIEW

Figure 33. Wood spring. Scale = full-size.

Lock back with pivot dowels in place.

STEP 13

Try the wood spring in the spring slot (Figure 32). Place a little glue on the end of the spring, or in the slot, and press the spring firmly into place. Center the spring in the slot. The top end of the spring should be about 3/16" from the top of the latch bolt slot (Figure 30).

STEP 14

The latch bolt is made of straight-grained pine or any other good wood.

Note: In detail "A" of Figure 34, the notch is wider at the top of the cutout than at the bottom. This allows the end of the spring to move when the latch bolt is retracted. The notch opening should be just big enough for the latch spring to slip in, but not tightly.

Sand the latch bolt just enough to smooth the saw marks. The latch must move freely back and forth in the latch slot.

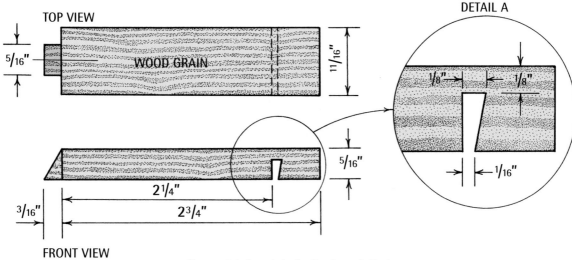

Figure 34. Latch bolt. Scale = full-size.

Center lamination cutout.

STEP 15

Carefully make a paper pattern of the lever. Transfer it to a piece of 3/4" wood. Make sure the wood grain is as shown in Figure 35.

STEP 16

I like to drill the 1/4" hole for the pivot first. Be sure to center it as shown.

Cut out the side view first and then cut the notch. This notch is where the key comes in contact, so sand it smooth. Round all edges slightly with sandpaper.

Make sure the lever is 1/16" thinner than the center lamination.

You should now have the lever and the latch bolt ready to install.

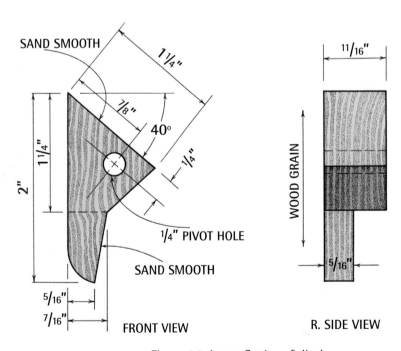

Figure 35. Lever. Scale = full-size.

STEP 17

Lay the back lamination on a flat surface. Lay the center lamination on top. Line up the sides and bottom, and clamp.

STEP 18

Place the lever on the pivot dowel. The lever must not bind on the pivot. If the spring does not rest on the spring stop (Figure 30), you must cut or sand a little off the face of the lever until it does. There should be a very small clearance between the spring and the lever.

STEP 19

Place the latch bolt in place. If the latch moves freely and projects into the shackle notch as shown in Figure 30, proceed to the next step. Quite often, the latch hits the spring stop and so it has to be shaved off a little with a knife or chisel. Also, you may have to shave a little off the dowel where the spring rests against it, to allow the latch to project a little farther into the shackle notch. The latch hitting the shackle when the lock is closed makes a nice "click" as it locks.

When the lever and the latch bolt work freely with no binding, remove the clamps and take the lock apart.

STEP 20

We are now ready to glue the lock together.

Turn the center lamination over and place a very small bead of glue on the arm above the latch bolt cutout. If glue squeezes out onto the latch bolt, the lock will probably be ruined. Apply glue to the remaining surface and carefully place the back lamination in place, lining up the sides and bottom.

Repeat the gluing procedure in step 20 on the face or top of the center lamination.

STEP 21

Place the latch bolt and lever in their proper places.

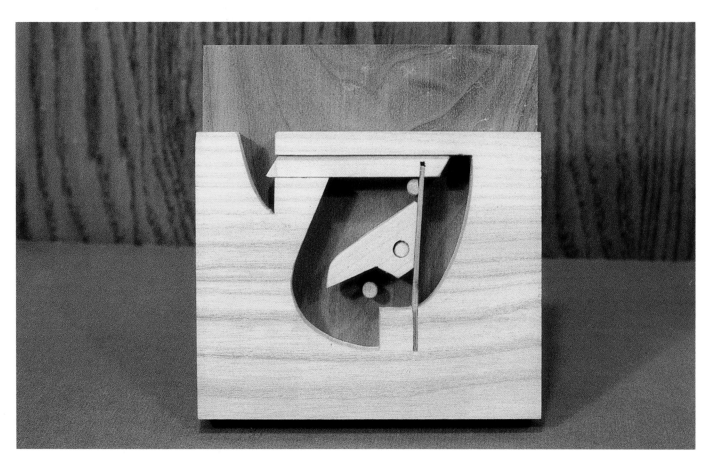

Lock back and center lamination with all interior parts.

STEP 22

Place the face on top, lining up the sides and bottom. Let the glue set a couple of minutes, then clamp down the assembly. Be careful not to move the pieces around. When fully clamped, push on the end of the latch bolt with a finger or dowel to make sure that the latch bolt moves freely. If not, take it apart quickly to see what the problem is.

STEP 23

Use Figure 30 to trace a pattern for the shackle. If you have not done so previously, make sure to mark the center of the shackle retainer pinhole. Transfer the pattern onto the piece of 3/4" wood that you chose for the shackle, making sure the wood grain goes up and down. Carefully saw out the shackle. I recommend that you do not cut a notch in the shackle for the latch bolt at this time.

STEP 24

Drill a 3/8" hole for the shackle retainer pin all the way through the shackle.

STEP 25

Sand the saw marks off with a drum or spindle sander. Smooth any uneven places so you have a nice even curve around the shackle.

On a belt sander, sand the sides nice and smooth, and sand down until the shackle slips into place between the ears on the lock top. There should be approximately 1/16" clearance. A little more clearance will not matter. Taper the sides at the latch end of the shackle as shown in Figure 36.

STEP 26

Drill a 1/2" recess in the shackle for the latch bolt, as shown in Figure 36, and cut out the end of the hole with a small chisel. Be careful not to split the end of the shackle or to cut completely through.

STEP 27

Refer to Figure 30 and mark where the router cuts stop on the edges of the shackle. Use a 3/16" roundover bit to round the corners. You may use a 1/8" or 1/4" bit if you like.

STEP 28

Put a 3/8" drill in the drill press and set it so that it comes down to 1/8" from the platform. Place the lock body in position and drill through the shackle retainer hole down to the stop. This hole will hold the shackle retainer pin in place.

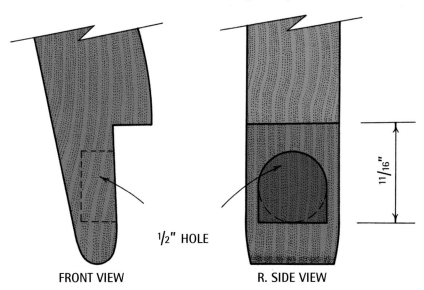

FRONT VIEW   1/2" HOLE   R. SIDE VIEW   11/16"

Figure 36. Shackle recess.

STEP 29

Cut a piece of 3/8" dowel 2" long to use for the shackle retainer pin. This dowel must turn freely in the hole in the shackle.

STEP 30

To make the key, saw out a piece of wood from the same kind of wood used for the shackle. Cut it 3/16" thick, 2" wide, and 6" or more long for easy handling.

Use a compass to make a 1-3/4" diameter circle on the 3/16" thick wood. Mark the center of the circle; bore the center hole with a 3/4" bit. Lay a piece of wood under your workpiece before drilling to minimize splintering the underside.

Cut another piece from the same 3/16" wood that is 5/8" wide and 7/8" long with. The grain of the wood should run in the long direction. We will call this piece the "bit" (Figure 37). Sand this piece and the finger piece smooth.

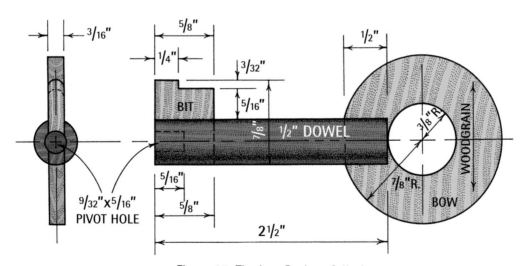

Figure 37. The key. Scale = full-size.

STEP 31

You may want to make a key jig to use on your band saw to hold the key shaft dowel while cutting the slot in each end (Figure 38).

You can use any piece of scrap wood for the base of the jig. Fasten two parallel strips 3/8" apart and high enough so that when the 1/2" dowel is laid in the groove it will not hit the base.

STEP 32

Cut a piece of 1/2" dowel 2-1/2" long for the key shaft. Make a straight pencil mark along one side of the key shaft dowel. Now make a mark 1/2" from one end and another mark 5/8" from the other end across this line.

Lay the key shaft in the jig with the long pencil mark at the center of the top.

Hold down firmly. Using your band saw, make a saw cut beside the line and stop at the cross mark 1/2" from the end. Keep making the cut wider until the finger piece just slips into the groove. Cut the slot in the exact center of the dowel.

Now make the 5/8" deep cut in the other end for the key bit. Make sure that the two cuts at either end of the dowel line up. If things do not come out right, make another dowel and try again.

STEP 33

Now glue the bit into the 5/8" notch in the key shaft. Make sure glue is on all parts that come together. Let the glue set completely. We will come back to the key later.

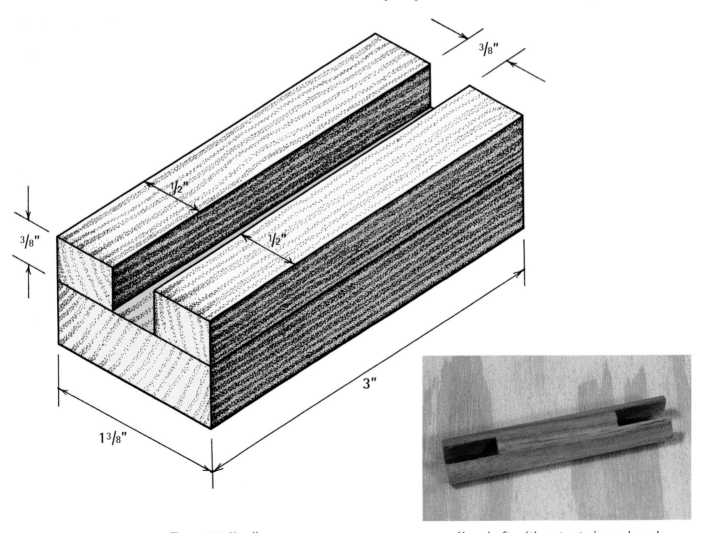

Figure 38. Key jig.

Key shaft with cutouts in each end.

STEP 34

Sand the front and back of the lock body smooth. Lay your pattern of Figure 31 on the lock body face. Using carbon paper, mark the outline onto the lock body, making sure your pattern doesn't move. Check the outline on the lock to ensure it is centered. If everything looks right, saw the outline on the band saw or scroll saw.

Smooth all saw marks with a drum or spindle sander. Make all curves nice and even. This is the shape of your finished lock.

STEP 35

If the lock back and face are made of 3/8" thick wood, use a 1/4" roundover bit in your router to round over the front and back edges. Check to make sure the bearing on the cutter does not run off the underside of the piece as you rout the top curves. If it does, use a smaller roundover bit.

STEP 36

Go back to the key now (Figure 37). Using a 9/32" bit, drill a 5/16" deep hole in the bit end of the key shaft. This hole must be in the center. Drill slowly so the drill does not split out the wood.

Turn the finger piece so the wood grain runs as shown and sand a flat place 1/2" long on one edge with the wood grain. This flat place fits the bottom of the slot in the key shaft. Place some glue in the slot at the end of the dowel shaft, and carefully press the finger piece into place. Wipe any excess glue off and let dry.

When the glue is set, mark the lever notch on the key bit (Figure 37), and cut a little wood from the notch. Note that the key bit is rounded over in the side view of the key.

STEP 37

Try the key in the lock, but do not force it. You may have to file or carve the keyhole a little bigger before the key fits.

When the key goes all the way in, it will turn. Again, do not force the key to turn. Your goal is to have the key turn clockwise about a half-turn, and stop against a stop that is built into the lever inside the lock. This is the unlocked position.

Work carefully to remove wood from the lever notch (Figure 37). Each time you turn the key, look in the shackle hole and watch the latch bolt retract. Fitting of the key should continue until, with the key turned to the stop, the latch is drawn back at least flush with the shackle hole.

Now install the shackle temporarily, and put the shackle retainer pin into place. Work the lock several times. Make sure the shackle does not bind or rub the sides. Sand and fit as needed to make it free. If the latch bolt does not snap into the shackle, remove the shackle and cut a little wood from the square end of the latch hole in the shackle until the lock works.

STEP 38

When the lock and key work properly, install the shackle and seat the retainer pin all the way in. Make a pencil mark at the lock face. Remove the pin and cut 3/16" shorter than the mark.

Remove the shackle pin and shackle.

STEP 39

Use the same kind of wood as used for the shackle to make the keyhole cover. Follow the dimensions in Figure 39 to lay out the shape of the cover and mark the center of the pivot dowel hole on the back.

Use a 1/4" Forstner bit to drill the pivot dowel hole into the back of the keyhole cover. Be careful not to drill through the face side.

STEP 40

Saw out and sand all edges, and the front and back to remove saw marks and scratches.

STEP 41

Use a compass to lay out two 1-1/4" diameter washers (Figure 39) on 1/8" plywood. Cut out and sand the edges until they just slide into the keyhole cover recess on the front of the lock with a little extra play.

Drill a 1/4" hole in the exact center of the two washers.

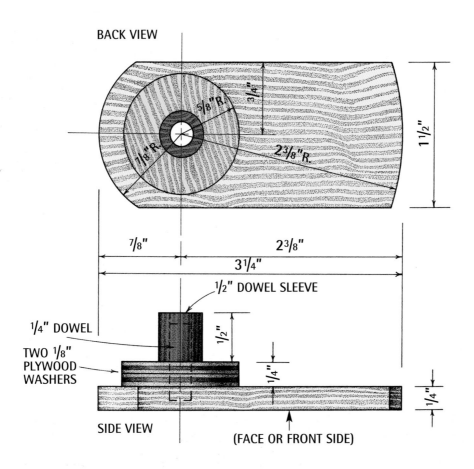

Figure 39. The keyhole cover. Scale = full-size.

STEP 42

Find a piece of 1/2" dowel about 1-1/2" long. Hold the dowel with a pair of pliers and drill a 1/4" hole in the center of one end, about 3/4" into the dowel. Now cut a 1/2" piece off the dowel with the 1/4" hole all the way through it.

Find a piece of 1/4" dowel that is snug, but not so tight that it will split the 1/2" dowel when inserted into the hole. Cut this dowel 7/8" long.

Try the 1/4" x 7/8" dowel in the holes of the two plywood washers. They should be just snug on the dowel also.

STEP 43

Now put a bead of glue on one end of the 1/4" dowel and push it into the hole in the keyhole cover.

Keyhole cover assembly.

STEP 44

Spread a little glue around the base of the dowel on the keyhole cover, and push one of the plywood washers onto the dowel, tight against the cover. Note: If the plywood washers have finish on one side, apply glue to the unfinished side since glue will not adhere to the finish material. Make sure the pivot dowel is perpendicular to the cover back. Let the glue dry before proceeding.

STEP 45

Slip the other plywood washer on the dowel without glue. Make sure to leave a side with bare wood exposed for gluing later.

Put a little glue in the 1/4" hole at one end of the 1/2" x 1/2" dowel. Do not put glue on the end of the 1/2" dowel. Press the 1/2" dowel onto the 1/4" pivot dowel so that it is snug against the washer. Make sure the 1/2" dowel is glued on. It holds the cover on the lock. Hold the second washer in your fingertips and turn the cover. It should turn with some resistance so that it will stay turned when moved, and does not fall back by itself.

The keyhole cover will not be glued in place until after the finish is applied.

STEP 46

Sand all exposed surfaces of the lock body, shackle, key, and keyhole cover. Sand with the grain of the wood. Keep sanding with finer sandpaper until you reach 220 grit.

Now select one 3/8" wood button to be glued in the hole in the lock face. I like to match the wood used for the shackle and keyhole cover.

Clean all the wood with a vacuum cleaner and wipe off with a tack cloth.

Drive four nails into a joist or other handy place for hanging the lock pieces to dry.

Start with the shackle. Hold it at the pivot hole and brush on the finish everywhere except where your fingers are. This will not show after assembly. Hang on a nail to dry.

The lock body should be finished from the top of the lock down. Do not under any circumstances let any finish get into the shackle hole. If it gets on the latch bolt, the lock will probably be ruined because the bolt will not work. You can hold the lock with your fingers for most of the finish application. Then finish the job by inserting the key, and holding the lock by the key to finish the job. Check for runs in the finish, smooth out, and hang the lock on a nail.

The keyhole cover should be finished front and back. Be very careful not to get any finish on the washers.

Place a piece of 1/4" dowel into the hole in the end of the key to hold it while putting on the finish.

Put finish on the head of the button.

When the finish has dried, sand all surfaces lightly with very fine sandpaper. Vacuum the wood and wipe it down again with a tack cloth. Then apply the second coat of finish.

You can add a third coat of finish if you like.

STEP 47

When the finish is completely dry, put a small bead of glue on one end of the shackle retainer pin, position the shackle, and push the dowel all the way in. It should be 3/16" below the face of the lock. This leaves room for the wood button.

Make sure the shackle opens and closes properly.

Try the button in the hole. If it is too tight, use the point of a sharp knife to take just a little off the edge of the hole. Use a nail to spread a little glue around the edge of the hole and tap the button tightly to the lock face.

STEP 48

Put a small bead of glue around the ledge of the keyhole cover recess and press the cover assembly into place. No glue should get on the outer washer or between them.

This completes the railroad switch lock.

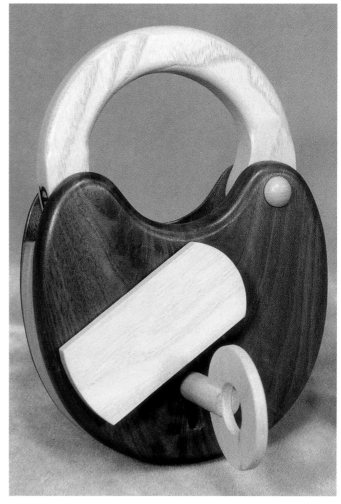

Finished railroad switch lock with key.

Chapter Nine
Antique Push Key Lever Lock, Or Pancake Lock, with Key

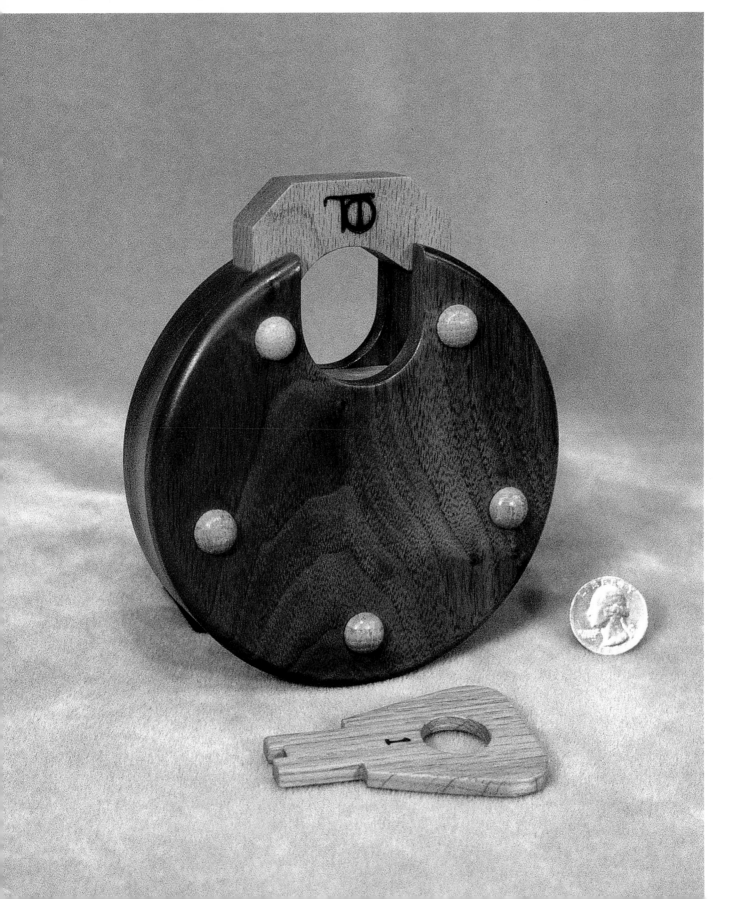

Push key lever locks were made from the 1800s to the early 1900s. They were a good lock and were made in great numbers. The lock that we will make now is designed to look and work like the metal lock.

STEP 1

Select the wood to be used for the lock body. If you have a band saw, which allows you to re-saw your wood, find a nice piece of figured hardwood for the front and back laminations. Saw two pieces 3/8" thick, 5-1/2" wide, and 5-1/2" long. These pieces must be square and cut to the exact size.

STEP 2

For the center lamination, use the same species of wood, but a piece with straight grain. Saw the piece 3/4" thick, 5-1/2" wide, and 5-1/2" long.

The shackle looks best if it is made of a contrasting wood. The five wood plugs on the face of the lock should be of the same kind of wood as the shackle.

STEP 3

Trace a pattern on paper using Figure 40, and mark the outside edge of the face piece. Locate the five hole centers ("A" through "E"), for the wood buttons. Mark the center of the lock face, the cutout for the shackle hole, and the outline of the finished lock.

If there is a smooth side to the face piece, turn it down. Make sure the wood grain runs the right way (Figure 40).

Place the pattern on the face of the lock and tape in position. Place carbon paper in between and mark the shackle hole, all five button hole centers, and the lock center.

You can use a compass to draw the lock outline, but be careful not to make a little hole where the compass pin rotates in the center, because it will show after the lock is sanded and finished.

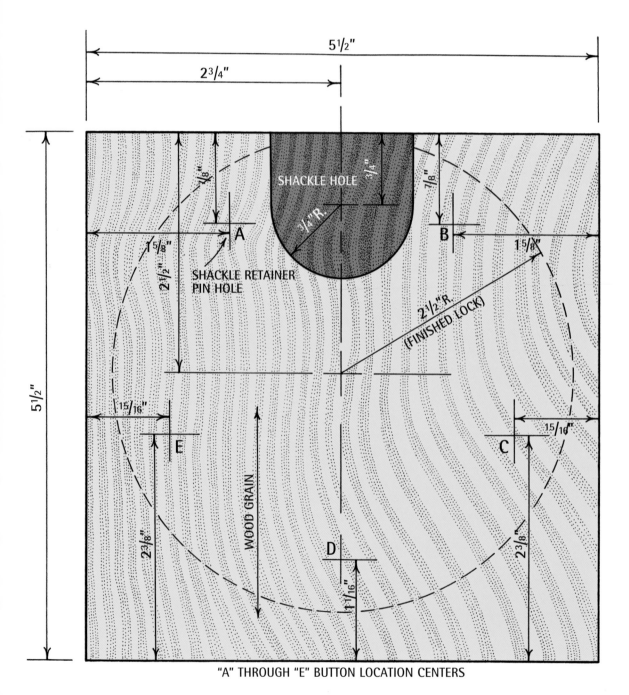

"A" THROUGH "E" BUTTON LOCATION CENTERS

Figure 40. Lock face piece. Scale = full-size.

STEP 4

Saw out the shackle hole, or bore out the round part with a 1-1/2" Forstner bit and finish the cut with a saw. Make this shackle cut in both the face and the back piece of the lock.

I recommend that you use a couple of small nails or brads driven in the corners, which will be cut off later, to hold the face and back pieces together while sawing out this notch. Cut the shackle hole. Then remove the brads and separate the front and back.

STEP 5

Now use a 3/8" Forstner bit to drill buttonhole "A" 3/16" deep into the face piece.

Reset the drill to cut 3/8" holes for buttonhole "B," "C," "D," and "E" to a depth of 1/4" into the face.

STEP 6

Use a 1/4" drill to drill all the way through buttonhole "A" in the exact center of the 3/8" recess hole.

Do not saw the lock outline now.

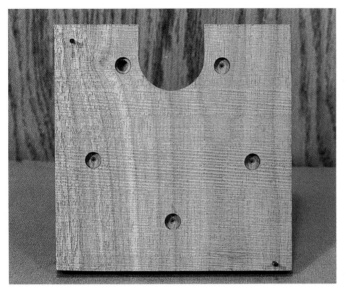

Front and back laminations with notch cutout.

STEP 7

Make a pattern of Figure 41, marking the outside edges, the shackle hole, and the three 1/4" dowel center locations. Make sure the dowels are accurately located.

STEP 8

Transfer the shackle hole and mark the dowel locations on the back piece, which has the smooth side turned up. Make sure the wood grain is turned right, and that the sides and bottom are even.

STEP 9

Next, using a 1/4" Forstner bit, drill the three dowel holes to within 3/16" of the other side of the back piece.

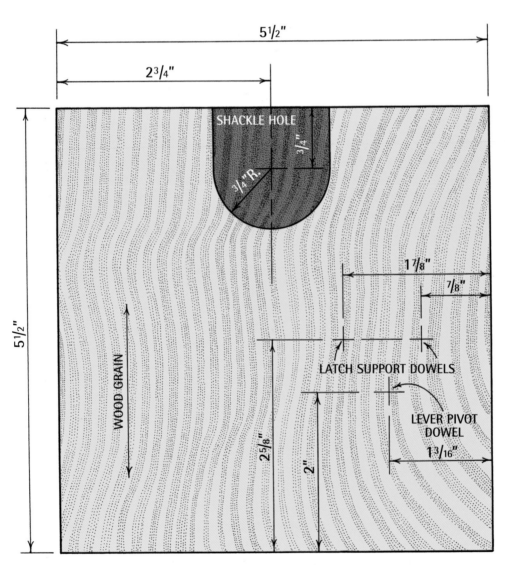

Figure 41. Lock back piece and dowel locations.

STEP 10

Make a pattern for the center piece from Figure 42 and transfer it to the piece that was cut out in Step 2. Again, check the direction of the wood grain.

Before you saw out the center lamination, drill a 1/4" hole through the bottom end of the key slot (Figure 42).

Note that the key slot will be open after the lock body is sawed out along the dotted line, which occurs after the lock body is glued together.

Saw out the inside very carefully. This piece is quite fragile at the top end of the spring notch and at the bottom of the key slot.

Sand the indicated areas smooth. These areas are exposed when the lock is completed and the shackle is opened and closed.

Center lamination cutout.

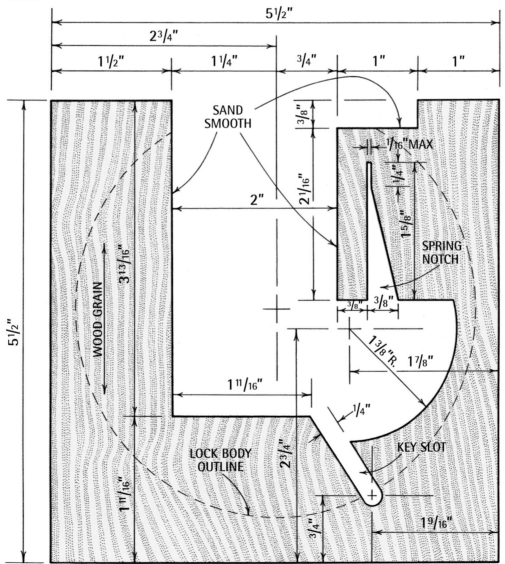

Figure 42. Lock center piece.

STEP 11

The latch spring is made of straight, fine-grained ash or hickory. It must be limber enough to bend 1/4" when the lock is opened. Fit it carefully into the spring notch (Figure 42). The spring should project 1/8" below the spring notch when in place. Glue the spring in place. You may have to glue a small shim with the spring to hold the spring in place. Make sure the spring is centered in the notch, and is against the straight side of the notch.

STEP 12

Now cut three pieces of 1/4" dowel to a length of 7/8" and glue them into the holes in the back lamination (Figure 41). Make sure they are perpendicular to the back.

STEP 13

Use a piece of fine-grained hardwood to make the latch bolt in Figure 44. As you can see, it is small and has some fine cuts in it.

Sand all sides and ends smooth and round the edges slightly.

Make a small piece, which we will call the "push bar," from a piece of fine-grained hardwood. This piece is 1/16" thick, 5/8" wide, and 3/8" long. The wood grain must run the 3/8" direction, as shown below. Glue the push bar into the 1/16" slot in the bottom of the latch bolt as shown in Figure 45.

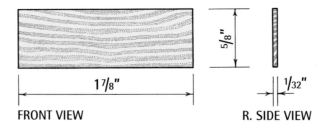

Figure 43. Latch spring. Scale = full-size.

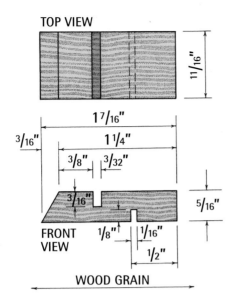

TOP VIEW

11/16"

1 7/16"

3/16"   1 1/4"

3/8"   3/32"

3/16"

FRONT
VIEW   1/8"   1/16"

1/2"   5/16"

WOOD GRAIN

Figure 44. Latch bolt. Scale = full-size.

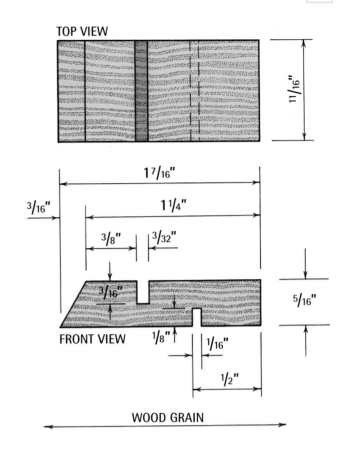

TOP VIEW

11/16"

1 7/16"

3/16"   1 1/4"

3/8"   3/32"

3/16"

FRONT VIEW   1/8"   1/16"

1/2"   5/16"

WOOD GRAIN

Figure 44. Latch bolt. Shown larger for clarity

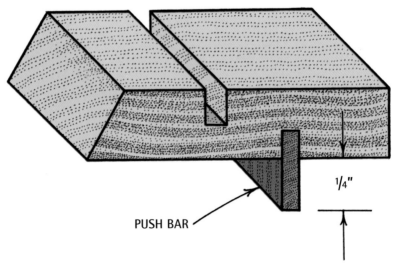

PUSH BAR

1/4"

Figure 45. Push bar.

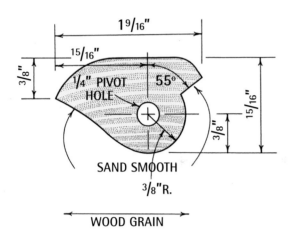

Fig. 46 Lever. Scale = full-size.

STEP 14

Trace the pattern at left and transfer it to a piece of hardwood that is 11/16" thick. Drill the 1/4" hole for the pivot dowel. Sand the two indicated areas smooth, and round all the edges slightly.

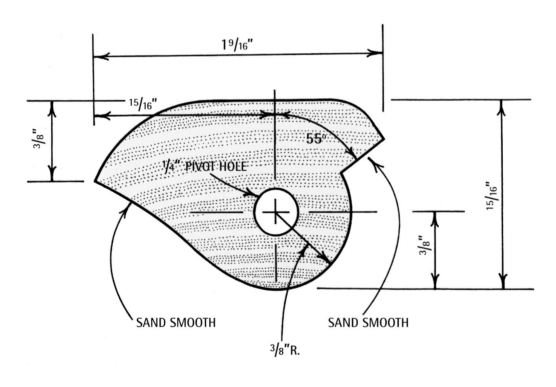

Fig. 46 Lever. Shown larger for clarity.

STEP 15

Make a pattern of the shackle from Figure 47, and transfer it to the piece of 3/4" wood you picked out for the shackle.

Saw out the wood on the band saw and then check to see if it will slide easily into the lock center section (Figure 42).

Sand the thickness of the shackle down so that it is at least 1/32" thinner than the center section. Then sand all edges and sides smooth.

STEP 16

Lay out the retainer pin notch on the shackle (Figure 47), and cut it out carefully with a chisel. This notch will have to slide along the shackle retainer pin after the lock is assembled.

Shackle ready to finish.

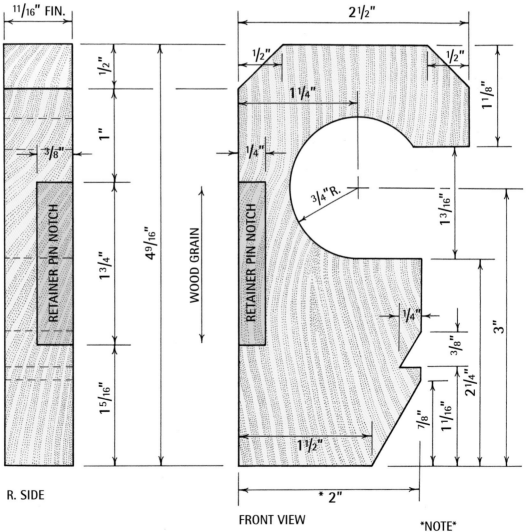

Figure 47. Shackle. (Not exact size.)

R. SIDE

FRONT VIEW

NOTE
THIS DIMENSION MUST FIT
INTO CENTER LAMINATION

STEP 17

Use a piece of the same kind of wood used for the shackle. Saw and sand to a thickness of 3/16" before cutting to length. Lay out the key as shown in Figure 48. The finger piece of the key can be any shape you like.

Drill out the 3/4" hole and then saw the outline. These cuts are not critical.

Sand all surfaces and round over all edges to your liking. The notch in the end of the key is only for looks.

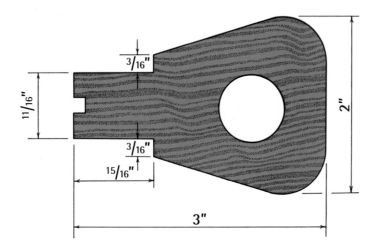

Figure 48. Key. Scale = full-size.

STEP 18

First you need to check the operation of the lock. Lay the back down and use two or three clamps to clamp the center lamination onto it, with the sides and bottom exactly even.

Place the latch bolt in place as shown below. You may have to shave a little off the support dowels to let the bolt slide freely.

Now slide the lever onto the lever pivot. You may have to enlarge the hole in the lever so that it moves freely.

When the latch bolt and lever are installed, they should look like the photo. Push on the lever to make sure it retracts the latch.

Rub paraffin on the end of the latch bolt and the angled part of the shackle bottom. This will make the lock work better.

Slide the shackle into place as if you are closing the lock. If the lock does not lock with a nice click, you need to do some fitting and sanding until the lock works properly.

Lock back and center laminations with all interior parts.

STEP 19

Remove the shackle, latch bolt, and lever.

Before you glue, look at the shape of the finished round lock, and determine where the glue will have to be spread. Note: Do not get any glue on the spring, lever, or latch bolt. Do not allow the glue to squeeze out onto these pieces when the lock body is clamped together. Use glue very sparingly anywhere close to the moving parts.

Now spread the glue on the back of the center lamination and place it carefully on the back lamination, lining up the sides and bottom.

Set the latch bolt and lever in place.

Spread glue on top of the center lamination, and place the face piece flush with the sides and bottom.

Clamp down carefully, making sure all pieces are lined up around the sides.

When the glue is fully set, refer to Figure 40 and lay out the lock body outline if you have not already done so.

STEP 20

Saw out the lock body on the band saw. Notice that the keyhole is now open.

Push the key into the keyhole while watching in the shackle hole. The latch bolt must retract fully. If not, do not put the shackle into the lock. You must adjust something.

Sand around the outside of the lock to remove the saw marks, and make a nice smooth curve. Sand the whole lock until ready for final sanding.

Use a 1/4" or 3/16" radius roundover bit to round the front and back corners of the body. Do not round over the shackle cutout edges with the router.

Slide the shackle into the lock to make sure that it is working.

Remove the shackle and do the final sanding of all the pieces.

You need five 3/8" wood buttons to finish along with the other parts.

STEP 21

Use a vacuum cleaner to clean all the parts inside and out. Wipe off the dust with a tack cloth.

Apply finish only partway down the shackle hole. Do not get any finish on the end of the latch bolt. Only finish the part of the shackle hole that shows when the shackle is open or closed. Make sure there are no runs in the finish.

After the finish is dry, lightly sand all surfaces with very fine sandpaper. Vacuum clean, and wipe with a tack cloth again.

Apply a second coat of finish.

STEP 22

To assemble, insert the shackle partway. Insert a 1/4" dowel into the retainer hole, then pull it back out just enough so that it does not rub on the shackle as it is moved up and down. Mark the dowel flush with the bottom of the retainer pin buttonhole, and cut to length. Place a little glue on the sides of the dowel (not on the end) and insert into the hole. Slide the shackle up and down to make sure the dowel does not rub.

Try each wood button in a hole. If the button is too tight, use the point of a sharp knife to remove a little wood from the edge of the hole. Spread a little glue around the edge of the holes and tap in the buttons.

This completes the push key lever lock.

I hope that you have enjoyed making these locks and that everyone who sees them, or receives one as a gift, will also enjoy them. Over the years that I have made and sold locks, I tell people that they are "conversation pieces," and become family heirlooms.

You can make the lock a special gift if you carve a name, birth date, anniversary, or retirement date into it. This adds a personal touch to your handcrafted wood lock.

Finished push key lever lock.

Chapter Ten
Gallery

Here are some additional locks, made using the techniques illustrated in this book. My hope is they inspire you in your own projects.

- Tim Detweiler *"The Lock Man"*

Screw key lock.

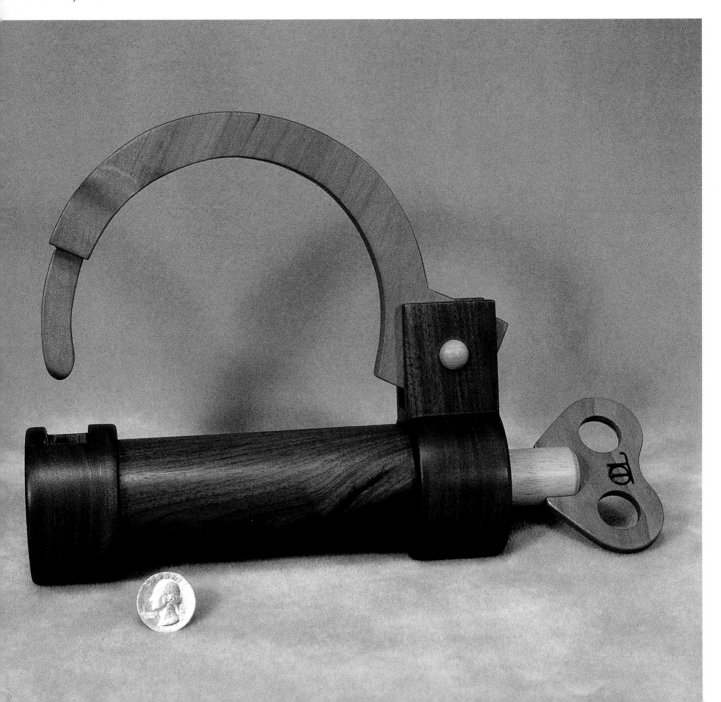

Combination lock with manzanita body.

Combination luggage lock.

Push button combination lock.

Warded lock with woods from all six continents that have trees.

Walnut and ash combination lock 10" x 16".

Cherry and walnut safe with three number combination lock, 11"w. 8"h. and 8"d.

Text and photography: Tim Detweiler
Drawings: James Goold
Editorial: Laura Tringali
Design and production: Morgan Kelsey